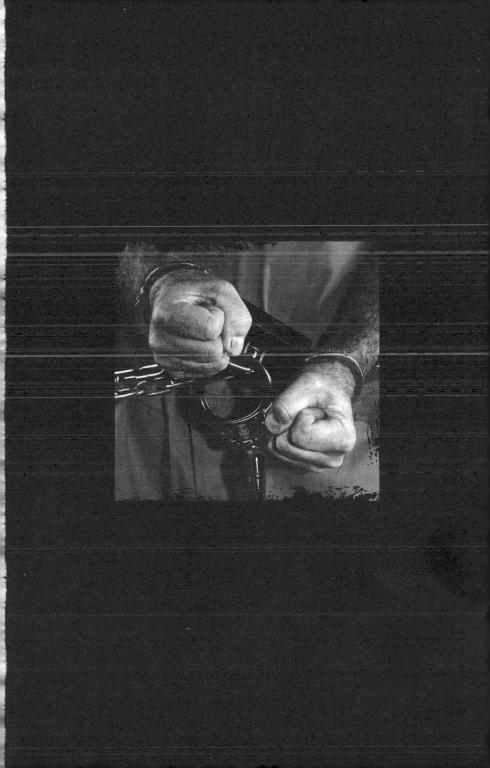

Welcome to Minnesota Correctional Facility–Oak Park Heights, a super-maximum-security prison housing the most violent and dangerous serial killers, murderers, drug dealers, and sex offenders.

These felons are not incarcerated here for singing too loud in church choir.

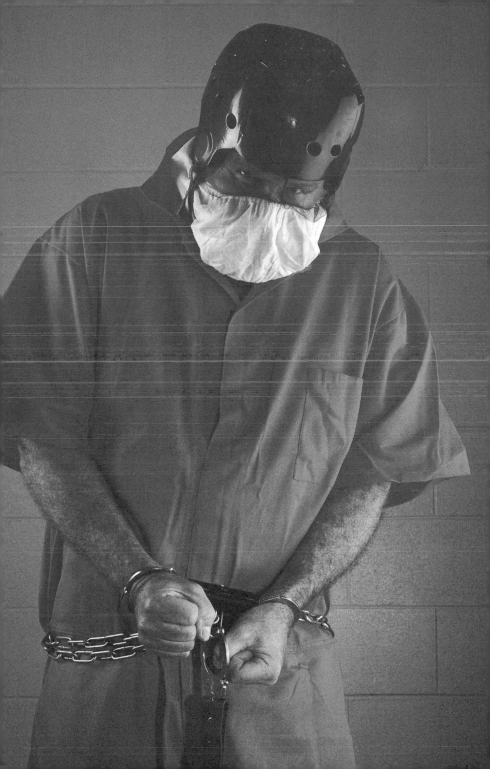

An inmate's cell measures seven by ten feet. Each contains a bed, table, toilet, and sink within the ambiance of reinforced-cement floors, walls, and ceilings. The bed is a cement slab topped by a thin mattress. The toilet is made of steel so it cannot be broken; it lacks the amenity of a hinged seat or a lid, which could be used as a weapon.

For inmates, this is home—sometimes for the rest of their lives.

In prison, nothing is as it seems.

On the outside, a bar of soap is for washing.

Inside, it becomes a deadly weapon if hidden in a sock and swung at someone's head.

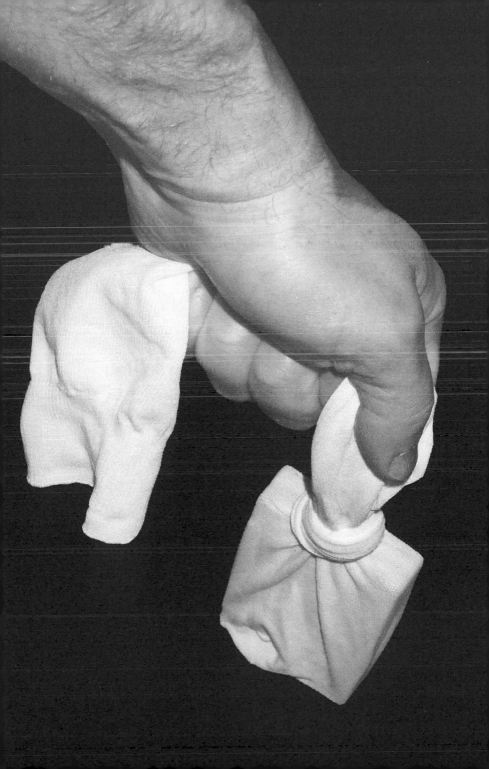

Outside, a toothbrush is for brushing teeth.

Inside, it can be sharpened into a homemade stiletto for settling disputes—once and for all.

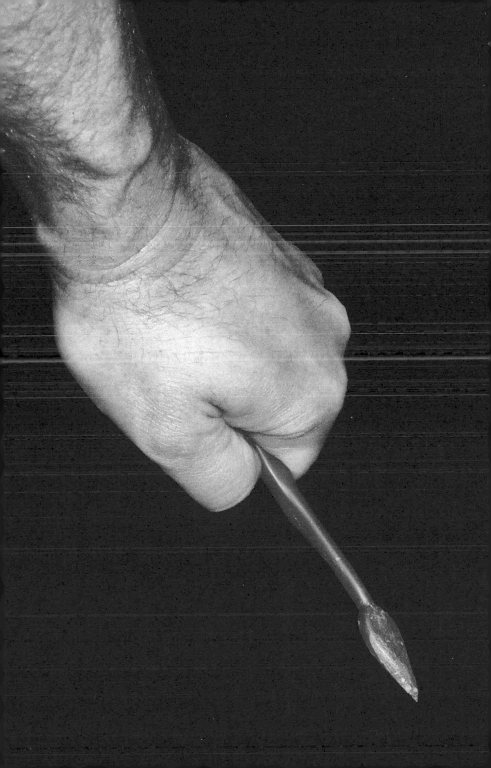

Outside, a Bible is a holy book.

Inside, it can be hollowed out and used as a cache for weapons or drugs.

BOOK I

Psalms 1–41

Psalm 1

Blessed is the man ª
who does not walk ᵇ in the counsel
of the wicked ᶜ
or stand in the way ᵈ of sinners ᵉ
or sit ᶠ in the seat of mockers. ᵍ
But his delight ʰ is in the law of the
LORD,
and on his law he meditates ʲ day
and night.

He is like a tree ᵏ plan[ted]
of water, ᵐ
which yields its fruit
and whose leaf ° does
Whatever he does p

[...] so the wicked!
They are like chaff ᑫ
[...]at the wind blows

⁵Therefore the wicked will not stand ʳ in
the judgment, ˢ
nor sinners in the assembly ᵗ of the
righteous.
⁶For the LORD watches over ᵘ the way of
the righteous,
but the way of the wicked will
perish. ᵛ

Psalm 2

¹Why do the nations conspire ª
and the peoples plot ʷ in vain?

[...] folly; [...]rth take their stand
[...]ing together

[...]inted One. ᵇ [...]
[...]ains, ²" they say,

1:1 ⁴S Dt 33:29;
Ps 40:4; 128:4
ᵇPs 89:15
ᶜS Job 21:16;
Ps 10:2-11
ᵈS Ge 49:6
ᵉPs 26:9; 37:38;
51:13; 104:35
ᶠPs 26:4
ᵍS Job 11:3;
Pr 1:22;
Isa 28:14; Hos 7:5
1:2 ʰPs 112:1;
119:16,35;
119:16,35;
Ro 7:22 ⁱPs 19:7;
119:1; Eze 11:20;
18:17
ʲS Ge 24:63
[...]ʲPs 52:8;
92:12; 128:3,
Jer 17:16; Zec 4:3

[...]pleasure accor[...]
[...]heering myself wi[...]
[...]ing folly—my mi[...]
[...] wisdom. I wanted[...]
[...]while for men to[...]
[...] the few days [...]

[...]at proje[...]
[...] and [...]
[...]dens[...]
[...]uit[...]

author and date unkno[...]
[...]e final outcome of the[...]
[...]v. 1) and "the way o[...]
[...] 37; Introduction to[...]
[...] introduction to the[...]
[...] that those of who[...]
[...]s) as the people of C[...]
[...]ince and favors wit[...]
[...]cterized by righ[...]
[...]them (v. 5; see [...]
[...]t speaks in the P[...]
[...] (and written) di[...]
[...] to blessedness.[...]
[...]ogressively (v[...]
[...]n in their ungod[...]
[...]se who revere the[...]
[...]19:1-2; 128:1[...]
[...]Isa 56:2), who [...]
[...]44:15; 146:5[...]
[...]34:8), and so[...]
[...]144:12-14; S[...]
[...]roclaiming the[...]
[...] all living thi[...]
[...]sanctuaries (J[...]
[...]nsel. Deliber[...]
[...]on oneself. s[...]
[...]for whom w[...]
[...]ckers. Thos[...]
[...](see Pr 1:22).[...]
[...]ditates. Seeking guidance for life in
the deliberations of the wicked. day

[...]not wither. See Jer 17:8; a simile of the
[...]teous. Such a tree withstands the
[...] flourishing, it blesses man, ani-
[...]ailing fruit and shade.
[...]vay. A simile of the wretchedness
[...] away by the lightest wind [...]
[...]leansing b[...]

[...]pleasure.
[...]h all my w[...]
[...]ord for all[...]

[...] that my [...]
[...]sdom without[...]
[...]God and [...]

2:1-3 The nations rebel. In the ancient Near East the
coronation of a new king was often the occasion for the
revolt of peoples and kings who had been subject to the
crown. The newly anointed king is here pictured as ruler
over an empire.
2:1-2 For a NT application see Ac 4:25-28.
2:1 Why . . . ?A rhetorical question that implies "How dare
they!"
2:2 LORD . . . his Anointed O[...]
Anointed is a[...]

[...]Y (as in 22:25; 26:12;
[...]Ps 15; 24). *righteous*.
[...]d's people; it presents
[...]order their lives in all
[...]man relationship they
[...]e relationship they
[...]ity (of whatever sort:
[...]religious, intellectual)

[...]destinies of the two
[...]ose who choose them.
[...]er and John ascribed it
[...]rdance with the Jewish
[...]primary author of the
[...]nally composed for the
[...]of the Lord's covenant
[...]etic words of judgment
[...]nouncements of God's
[...]gh an exalted royal son
[...]mport of this psalm. As
[...]uction to the Psalms, it
[...] acknowledge the lord-
[...]ke refuge in him" (v. 12;
[...]piety that speaks in the
[...]oted in the NT, where it
[...]on of David and God's

[...]; 89:5; 102:32; 111:1;
[...] Na 1:7 ˢS Lev 26:38;
2:2 ²Ps 48:4
2:3 ⁴S Job 36:8

2 Or anointed one

The BIG HOUSE

Life Inside a Supermax Security Prison

Warden James H. Bruton

Voyageur Press

Life Inside the Razor Ribbon

This football game was different from any other ever played.

The game wasn't over when the clock ran out or when one team scored in overtime. It didn't end with a record-setting field goal or a long touchdown pass. This game ended when the quarterback stabbed the running back.

It was a glorious summer day on the field, the green grass aglow in the sunlight and the crowd cheering on the players. Yet this wasn't playground or recreation football, nor was it a college or professional game. The players were serial killers and drug dealers, rapists and child molesters, murderers and thieves, convicted felons who had committed atrocious acts against innocent victims. Their field of play was different from the grassy public parks, sandy lots, or stadiums that host most games. The gridiron was in the yard at the super-maximum-security Minnesota Correctional Facility-Oak Park Heights. This was prison, a place that brings together men with histories of settling their differences with violence. The Big House—an environment of myth and mystery behind high walls, a place the outside world tries to ignore yet watches with intrigue.

On the surface the football field was largely the same as any other, with team benches, yard markers at regulation distances, goalposts, and end zones. But instead of spectators in stands, press boxes, and luxury suites, correctional officers with Colt M15 automatic rifles observed from the rooftop and brick walls were laced with sensor systems, creating an air of foreboding not found at other stadiums.

The Oak Park Heights complex is made up of eight housing units in a circular pattern surrounding the eight-acre recreation yard. Each unit contains fifty-two of Minnesota's most aggressive, dangerous, and violent prisoners. As its first warden, Frank Wood, once told me, "These people are not here for singing too loud in church choir." Each team in this game was the home team and no one left the stadium when the game was over. In fact, some stayed behind for years, some for the rest of their lives.

It was the prison's recreation schedule and incentive-based program rewarding good behavior that had brought members of two housing units to the yard to play football on this particular Saturday afternoon. Yet in the Big House, past good behavior doesn't always dictate future good behavior. This truth would certainly be demonstrated today.

The offense came out of the huddle and lined up in formation as on any other play. The center snapped the ball and the quarterback turned to hand off to the running back for a rush to the right. But the quarterback did not execute the play as called.

Outside prison walls, when a quarterback changes the play at the line of scrimmage it's called an audible. From an inmate's perspective, changing the play on this day was called taking care of business. Some quarterbacks carry a card with notated plays, others a wristband with their notes. The quarterback in this game carried a piece of non-regulation equipment—a sharpened length of metal known as a "shank," prison slang for a crude homemade knife. He wasn't concerned with moving the ball down field or winning the game. His goal was doing in one of his own teammates.

Instead of handing off the ball, the quarterback plunged the shank into the running back's chest. No routine handoff, this was a premeditated assault with a deadly weapon. The ball tumbled to the ground and the field of play erupted in chaos.

This game was over.

✦✦✦

The quarterback was John Albus, a felon with plenty of prison years behind him and a long sentence still ahead. He had been transferred to Oak Park Heights for causing trouble at another prison and was labeled as "high risk." Yet for some time his behavior had been exemplary, qualifying him to live in the special unit whose inmates had been rewarded with this game. But it was all one big con. Albus had likely planned his attack months in advance. For him, feigning good behavior, getting into the special unit, and playing football were all part of a larger game with deadly intent.

After the attack, we immediately sounded a Code Three. Over our prison radios, staff was alerted that there was an inmate-on-inmate assault with a weapon. The special Security Squad ran double-time to the yard. Made up of highly trained and experienced officers, the Security Squad is the Big House equivalent of a police SWAT team, adept at managing any kind of disturbance thrown at them. The squad leader first gave orders to clear the yard, sending all the players back to their cells for a lockdown. The Security Squad blitzed the quarter-back, sacked and handcuffed him. They then hustled him off to the Segregation Unit—his football career was over. During this action, emergency response personnel attended to the injured running back. The weapon, however, had disappeared.

We quickly made several important discoveries. The game had been videotaped by an inmate so it could be played on closed-circuit TV for the rest of the prisoners. While recording the play-by-play action, the inmate also captured the deadly final play. As soon as the camera operator realized he had recorded an assault, he immediately tried to destroy the tape. No self-respecting inmate would ever assist the staff in any-thing—especially providing evidence in an attack. The staff members, however, were quicker on their feet. We intercepted the tape intact, and it became key evidence during the quarterback's ensuing criminal trial.

The clarity of the game tape would have done Monday Night Football proud, and the bright sunlight proved critical in providing a piece of evidence. Without the actual weapon, we could not produce physical evidence linking the perpetrator to the assault. All we had was a victim who had been stabbed in the gut with something—and that something definitely wasn't a football. But the videotape clearly showed that as the quarterback turned to hand off what appeared to be the ball to the running back, a sudden flash appeared on the tape. Reviewing the play, we determined that flash to be the sun glinting off metal. The videotape and that brief, shining flash proved to the court the precise time of the stabbing and that a weapon had been used.

Weapons are made in prison with mind-boggling imagination. A scrap of metal, a piece of hard plastic, a chair leg, a broken wastebasket, a sliver of wood—all are raw material for prisoners to form into dangerous weapons. Plastic and wood are ideal because they won't be picked up by a metal detector. Small objects are coveted as they can be easily hidden in the mouth to be carried about within prison. Serious assaults have been made with just a bar of soap held in a sock and swung with powerful force. Pencils or toothbrushes rubbed to razor-sharp points become stilettos. Ingenuity is the key ingredient, revenge the mother of invention. It's an art, in a strange sort of way, and inmates are masters.

It would have been tough to smuggle the weapon out of the unit hidden in clothing, as officers always search inmates before they enter the yard. That yard is also searched by staff after its use, so hiding an object outside would require cunning.

The problem is that cunning is part of the inmate mindset—the tougher the challenge and the tighter the security, the better they become at ways to defeat it. Inmates carry weapons if they can—they believe they may need them for their own protection or to do someone in. Hiding a weapon inside the rectum is a common way to move contraband inside a prison; keeping drugs or other secret items on a temporary basis in this personal hiding place may not be comfortable, but inmates consider it a necessary evil. It's also almost impossible to detect. A seasoned con has nothing but time on his hands to deceive, manipulate, and orchestrate underhanded activity with the precision of a brain surgeon.

I never found out how the shank got onto the football field and into the quarterback's possession. It may have been smuggled into prison specifically for this assault. The quarterback might have made the weapon in the industry shops, brought it to the living unit, and eventually into the yard secreted on his person or in his clothes. Or another inmate may have smuggled it in for him. The weapon may have been hidden in a secure spot in the yard for some time. There could have been several others involved in shifting the contraband from person to person prior to the assault.

The weapon was never found. The attacker and his likely accomplices had prepared for hiding and disposing of it before prison screws—inmate slang for correctional officers—got their hands on it.

I also didn't have a clue what might have been the motive for the stabbing. Was it a gambling debt, or perceived disrespect? Was it a dispute over drugs? Was it over now, or would there be repercussions?

I struggled to answer the question of how long in advance the stabbing had been planned. The setting in the recreation yard was the perfect playing field for the attack, as the cons were grouped close together making it difficult to identify participants. How many knew what was going to occur? If the players know the play is to be a stabbing, do the ends complete their routes, do the tackles block? Does the defense try to sack the quarterback if they know he has a weapon he's ready to use? There's an unwritten code that prisoners provide no credible information to officers. Even though the stabbing threatened his life, the running back kept mum. Whatever the reason for the attack, he got the message loud and clear.

I've been around college and professional football myself, but nothing could prepare me for the Big House. Before choosing corrections as a career, I played Big Ten football with the University of Minnesota Golden Gophers and practiced in pro training camps with the 1968 Dallas Cowboys and 1967 and 1971 Minnesota Vikings. By the time I became Oak Park Heights warden in 1996, I thought I knew football and prisons. I've seen the biggest, toughest pro athletes imaginable, but I had never seen football played Big House style.

When you walk inside the walls of a supermax prison, you are entering a bizarre new world. There are many incidents so foreign to the outside they almost seem make-believe. It's a fantasy world rife with drama and deception, unlike anywhere else on earth.

I often wonder what the average citizen would say about this world if he or she were exposed to it for a lengthy period of time—or even for just one night in a cell. Prison tours bring you inside where you can observe security procedures and inmates at work or study. Even a morning tour can be an education for those that have never been inside the walls. A short visit, however, is only a snapshot of what really goes on in this world.

What's missing from this small glimpse is the prison culture and all of the mystery that goes with it. A tour would likely never come upon a stabbing in the yard or ever really understand the industry of smuggling drugs. Illicit tattooing, gangs, inmate hierarchy, contraband weapons—you'll see none of these.

Life as a warden or prison officer is different from most any other job in any other workplace. Every morning, I would meet with my staff to review the reports from each post on all three shifts, documenting the previous day's activities. This gave us an opportunity to appraise problems—and it was rare that there wasn't a problem. On any given morning we might discuss separating two inmates so they wouldn't slit each other's throats, searching food carts for contraband drugs, or locking down cells as a precaution to prevent a riot. One day, I decided we must bolt together the prison chapel's chairs and benches. That Sunday morning a fight had erupted during church services, and inmates had used their chairs as weapons. Bolting the chairs together was a simple solution to stop them from being thrown during chapel brawls, although determining why the incident happened and how to prevent it from occurring again was more difficult. I teased our chaplain that he presided over the only church where the pews were bolted together so the congregation couldn't throw them at each other. He didn't seem to appreciate my sense of humor.

Inmates incarcerated at Oak Park Heights have dangerous pasts—pasts that usually follow them into prison. The lessons they've learned in life on the outside are just transferred to the inside. The majority of prisoners are murderers or have committed other violent crimes, and violence is usually the only way they know how to deal with issues. I'm always bewildered and alarmed by the willingness of many inmates to hurt or kill someone over something as trivial as a gambling debt or a minor misunderstanding. Their reasoning and logic are often distorted—even perverse—making each day a challenge.

Sometimes it is difficult to determine what is real in this world and what isn't. A fight between two inmates may be exactly what it seems—or it may be something else altogether. The fight might have been staged to divert the prison staff's attention from what's happening elsewhere. Contraband found in one unit may have been planned to be found so inmates could secure their concealment of something else.

I often wondered if anything was real.

Being in control of a supermax prison is like playing football on a grand scale, but instead of playing for champagne and a Super Bowl ring, you're playing for lives. Every day you try to stay one step ahead of your opponent. The mentality of us versus them exists at every moment, underlying every activity. I once overheard an inmate telling other cons it was his job to do what he could to break the rules and it was our job to catch him—if we could. This is the reality of prison. It's a game of its own, inmates versus officers, and we're all playing for keeps.

One of the realities of running a prison is taking calculated risks. I once took a risk with an inmate that could have cost people their lives. Charlie Vaughan was a triple murderer; the third victim had been his girlfriend. He was a large man, standing six feet eight inches tall, weighing 260 pounds, and was serving a sentence of life without parole. And we took him home on a Friday night.

You read right: We took him out of one of the most secure prisons in the world and brought him home.

Minnesota's Department of Corrections has a long-standing policy allowing for deathbed and funeral visits. Thus, depending on an inmate's behavior, we may allow a three-time killer to go to the deathbed of an immediate family member or attend a funeral. Vaughan's father was dying at home and the inmate had requested to see him. We had a tough decision to make.

On the face of it, the decision may seem an easy one. Take a triple-murderer out of a supermax prison to visit home? The very idea was ridiculous. Yet the more I thought about it, the more it seemed the humane thing to do—even though Vaughn's own history proved he had no deep-seated love for humanity.

To minimize the risk, we began thorough planning and preparation. When we were ready—and without telling the inmate any details so he couldn't make escape plans—we brought Vaughan to our holding room in the prison intake area. He was handcuffed and shackled with chains that were locked together at his waist; we then transferred him to a prison security vehicle and set out. With the assistance of the Correction Department's Special Investigation Unit and local law enforcement, we took him home guarded by twelve staff members in eight vehicles.

The inmate's trip home went smoothly. After a brief visit, Vaughan was brought back to prison. His father died the next morning.

The deathbed visit meant a lot to Vaughan, his parents, and even to neighbors, who remarked on the compassion shown the family. And although it was not part of our motive, that death-bed visit may pay for itself in other ways. Someday there may be an incident, and hopefully, this offender will remember the compassion shown him in a time of need. Down the road, that deathbed visit could save the life of an officer.

It was a calculated risk with grave consequences, and I'm still haunted by visions of what could have gone wrong. I'll never forget that, and I think the inmate will always remember what the staff did for him and his family. These kinds of decisions don't exist in the business community outside the walls of supermax prisons. For a warden, a decision like this comes with the job. Sometimes you make the right one. Next time, maybe not.

My daily interactions with inmates run the gamut from the simply strange to the truly terrifying. These interactions are skewed from the start because on most days in most situations, inmates lie. It's a generalization, a stereotype—but it's been proven over and over again. Lies, misrepresentations, distortions, and half truths are the norm. Little an inmate says is ever believed without full verification. It's unfortunate, but true. It's also unfair to those few offenders who do tell the truth. When you are responsible for a prison, you soon realize this may be the sole profession where you start off every conversation with your "client" assuming they are not going to tell you the truth.

I was superintendant of another correctional facility when inmate Ellis Wayne broke down in tears as he told me he'd just learned his sister had been gunned down, the innocent victim of a grocery-store robbery. He was distraught, and for the next two days, the staff counseled him and handled him with compassion as he grieved his loss. I have always been proud of my officers' humaneness when an inmate has a crisis in his family. Our chaplain, watch commander, caseworker, and others assisted this inmate through a tough time while we also made arrangements for him to attend the funeral.

Yet as the final plans were being set, the caseworker confided to me that because he couldn't locate where the victim's body had been taken after the shooting, he was having difficulty finding when and where the funeral was to take place. We investigated further and discovered there hadn't been a shooting at all that day, not even a grocery-store robbery. Something was wrong.

I had the inmate brought to a private room and confronted him. His grief, tears, and emotional distress dissolved. The slain sister was alive and well. He had made up the whole story. I grilled him on his motives, and surprisingly, he was happy to confess the truth. He told me he was bored and wanted something to do. He had enjoyed his acting role and the compassion the staff offered him. He liked controlling us and secretly laughed at the work we went through trying to set up a visit to a funeral that didn't exist. He wanted to have some fun for a couple of days at our expense. Now he was basking in the glory of making us jump through hoops and felt no remorse for his actions.

For me and my staff, the whole event was disheartening, the inmate's motives demented. And yet—inside institutional walls, behind the rolls of razor ribbon, the cons and cunning, the lies and deceptions, and the never-ending games inmates play—it was all part of a normal workday.

The Most Secure Prison on Earth

At the dawn of the 1970s, American prisons were hellish institutions and prisoners were ready for revolt.

Conditions were deplorable and inmates' rights neglected. It all erupted on September 13, 1971, at New York's Attica prison when an insurrection broke out. Inmates took control of the prison's D Yard and held staff members hostage for four long days. Finally, Governor Nelson A. Rockefeller decided enough was enough. He ordered in a military assault, sending a helicopter to drop tear gas on the prisoners. Then, one thousand state troopers stormed the yard, firing indiscriminately on the unarmed prisoners. In the end, thirty-nine lay dead, nine of them hostages.

The Attica revolt awakened the United States to prison issues long simmering on the edge of open violence. The country was soon torn between inmates' rights and a call for a tough hand to regain order.

The mood in Minnesota's state prison at Stillwater was similarly dangerous. In 1953, a major riot started in Stillwater prison protesting conditions and rules. The riot became so vociferous that residents in the nearby town of Bayport reportedly could hear the inmates shouting. In 1960, prisoners revolted again and had to be forced back into their cells at bayonet point by 150 guards. Later that year, another uprising was quelled with tear gas.

A dramatic escape attempt was foiled in 1970. Three Stillwater officers were taken hostage by inmates, who dressed in their uniforms and attempted to walk out the gates. At the same time, other inmates tried to cut through bars but were halted when the warden fired a shotgun blast into their cellblock. Later that year, another uprising was stopped by officers using shotguns and tear gas. In 1971, a deranged inmate stabbed the warden several times. Disturbances recurred during 1972, 1973, 1974, and 1975, prompting the Minnesota State Legislature to investigate conditions at the state prison.

In 1976, Frank W. Wood was made warden at Stillwater. He decided it was time for staff to retake control of the prison and run it in a safe, secure, and most importantly, humane manner. Wood began unannounced cellblock searches, confiscating a growing pile of weapons and contraband from the inmates. In the end, officers hauled several truckloads of contraband out of Stillwater.

Wood started as a prison officer in the late 1950s at Stillwater and worked his way through the ranks to eventually head the Minnesota Jail Inspection and Enforcement Unit. From this post, he was appointed Stillwater warden, and he immediately began his campaign of turning a troubled facility into one of the nation's best prisons. It was Wood's vision that laid the foundation for the Minnesota Correctional Facility-Oak Park Heights supermax prison that opened under his command in 1982.

Inmates incarcerated at Oak Park Heights have dangerous histories and are classified as high risk. In addition to housing Minnesota's most dangerous offenders, Oak Park Heights also holds maximum-custody inmates from other states and the Federal Bureau of Prisons. For more than twenty years, Oak Park Heights has had the largest contract in the nation to house federal prisoners, bringing more than $50 million dollars of income to Minnesota in the past two decades. Offenders transferred here by the Federal Bureau of Prisons didn't just write bad checks or steal cars. Rather, they are individuals with long violent histories who have usually spent years in supermax isolation.

On a cloudless day, sunlight sparkles off the massive walls of razor ribbon and double layers of sensor-controlled cyclone fencing surrounding the Oak Park Heights prison's 160 acres.

Several of the living units are built into the hillside with roofs at ground level. An eight-acre plot cut out of the middle of the adjoining walls makes up the secure recreation yard.

The secure recreation yard—a desolate place in wintertime.

A sweat lodge built by Native American inmates within the secure recreation yard.

You can best view the Oak Park Heights facility from the air. Flying above the St. Croix River Valley, you look down on the rolling prairie grasslands leading up to the wide swathe the river cuts into the hillsides. Nestled into these hills is Oak Park Heights prison, constructed largely below ground in an earth-sheltered facility.

Entering the prison from the main road to the west, you may initially think you've taken a wrong turn to the administration building of a school or headquarters of a corporation. Even within the front lobby there are no indicators you have entered a supermax correctional facility.

Only after you pass through the secure perimeter and travel downward four levels below ground do you realize you're in a place where the most dangerous humans on earth live. The first clues come at four separate security doors that have to be opened by an officer in the Master Control Center. The security clearance, hum of electronic sliding doors, and loud bang of door locks opening and closing let you know you are entering the strange world of prison. An instructor in our education unit once told me that to reach his classroom, a correctional officer had to open eight separate doors. No wonder I often stand by doors at home waiting for someone to open them for me.

There are two sets of corridors within the prison: one for staff alone and one shared between staff and inmates. The shared corridor surrounds the facility. The tiled floor is spotless, buffed to a magnificent shine. The walls are gray-painted concrete. As you walk the giant circle around the prison, the path seems endless. The walk can be long, quiet, and lonely.

An inmate's cell measures seven by ten feet. Just a few footsteps will take you from wall to wall, corner to corner.

This is the limit of an inmate's freedom.

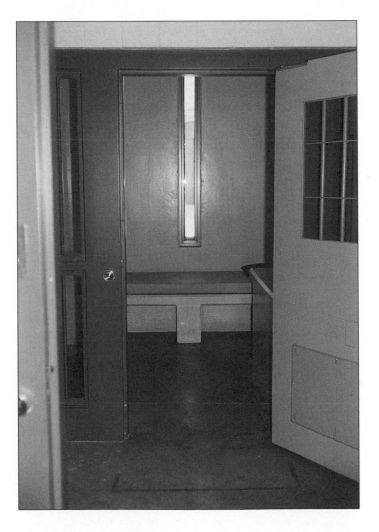

Each cell has one rectangular window. This window is tall and thin, and designed to be too narrow to escape through—should an inmate first be able to break the reinforced glass and squeeze around the steel-reinforced cement mullions.

A cell is a room with a view, but the window looks out into the prison's enclosed central yard tucked inside the walls, solidifying the concept that breaking out of a cell would be breaking deeper into the prison.

The marked area is the sole space within their cell that inmates are allowed to affix pictures or posters.

The toilet is in a corner. It's made of steel so it cannot be broken. It also lacks a seat—which could be broken off and used as a weapon.

An officer monitors the prison's sensors, video cameras, and audio surveillance from the main control center.

View of a two-story cellblock, with cell doors at right.

The cellblocks are rarely peaceful. During the day, there is the sound of banging doors and clicking locks. Even in the dark, the noise often continues. Sometimes yelling, screaming, and swearing echo down the halls throughout the night.

Cleanliness is a high priority at Oak Park Heights. The prison today is as clean and well kept as the day it opened. That physical appearance sets the tone for everything else within, establishing an internal pride among the staff that is contagious to all of the prison's operations and expectations.

I've had the opportunity to visit numerous prisons across the country, many of which were poorly run. The quality of the prison operation was always in direct correlation to the cleanliness inside and outside the facility. Some years ago, I visited a prison in Missouri that was filthy throughout and obviously dreadfully managed. The staff looked and acted unprofessional and seemed to have only tenuous control over the inmates. Cellblocks and cells were unkempt, and a prevailing attitude of hostility existed in most areas. I couldn't wait to get outside and breathe free air. It was not a safe institution and, in my opinion, a scary place to live in, work in, or even visit. On another occasion I toured a relatively new institution in Nevada. It was an unpleasant experience in a poorly managed facility. In the Segregation Unit, I found garbage had been stacked up outside cells, then thrown and strewn about the unit. The floors were filthy, the walls and railings going up to the upper tier of cells marred and scratched. Everywhere the mood was volatile. Inmates were banging on their doors, threatening guards. The prison had taken on the character of its appearance.

That the appearance of a prison tells something about its character is usually true for well run, safe institutions too. They are generally clean and organized. There is no excuse for anything short of absolute cleanliness, polish, and professionalism. It is critical. Oak Park Heights set the model and has managed it to perfection.

Over the years, I have heard complaints from the public that the prison is too comfortable and clean for inmates. People ask, Why do killers, rapists, robbers, and sex offenders get to live in such a pleasant, well-groomed surrounding? It doesn't seem right, they imply. Without even getting into the treatment of inmates, I wonder if the public actually expected the state to construct a $31.8-million prison and then let it fall into ruin.

More importantly, the cleanliness at Oak Parks Heights reflects the prison's philosophy. It all starts with how people are treated. Minnesota's corrections philosophy begins with the understanding that an offender's punishment is being in prison; it's not the responsibility of prison staff to continue the punishment beyond incarceration. This concept forms the foundation of the operating principles, creating a positive environment from the beginning.

A number of corrections officials from other states and many foreign countries have visited and toured Oak Park Heights since it opened in 1982. The impressive physical plant, unique earth-sheltered complex, and high-tech security are attractions, but most of the attention is focused on the incentive-based programming. Allowing high-risk inmates out of their cells for most of the day is not the norm for operating prisons.

Most maximum-security and supermax prisons isolate all offenders in their cells twenty-three hours a day. The prison's mission then demands little, if any, programming. The daily hour when inmates are out of confinement is usually spent in an enclosed and secure area, isolated again from human contact. Interaction with staff or other inmates is rare.

Offenders classified to this custody level are determined to be too dangerous to be out of their cells for any length of time, and therefore, total control and solitary confinement is believed to be the sole solution. This may be true for certain offenders, but not for an entire prison population. Even for the few who have shown they must be securely confined, incentives must be in place to reward positive behavior.

During the past decade, entire supermax isolation prisons have been built across the United States housing hundreds—and in some states, thousands—of inmates. The "supermax" label identifies facilities housing the worst of the worst in total and complete isolation.

This philosophy cares little for an inmate's eventual release back into the community. After long-term confinement and the loss of hope for offenders controlled under these conditions, mental deterioration is almost assured. The supermax total-isolation concept maintains security to the highest degree, but is it the humane way to treat people? And most importantly, does it provide the rehabilitation necessary for the majority of offenders who will someday be released to the community? Would you want someone living for months or years in these conditions to be released someday to live next door to you? Would you want to stand in line next to them in a grocery store or sit next to them in a movie theater?

I know I wouldn't.

Of course to have any credibility, there has to be a track record to support Oak Park Heights's unique corrections philosophy. To review a prison's history, there are six identifiable aspects of daily life that can be evaluated: the number of homicides that have taken place in the prison, number of escapes, use of drugs, presence of weapons, active role of gangs, and, finally, is it safe to walk through any area of the prison with inmates present?

Oak Park Heights's grades are unmatched.

In more than twenty years of operation, there has never been a homicide at Oak Park Heights.

In more than twenty years of operation, there has never been an escape.

Drugs are generally prevalent in prisons, but at Oak Park Heights they are infrequent at best. It takes committed staff to control their use through regular searches and proper security procedures. Urinalysis testing is done regularly, and there have been periods where testing has gone for as long as two years without drugs being present. This is unheard of in most prisons.

Homemade weapons, so common in most prisons, are rarely found at Oak Park Heights and not likely to be used in combative occurrences among the inmates. Most of the disagreements involve yelling and occasionally punches. Since weapons must be prevented from being made or confiscated immediately, strong policies and procedures requiring routine and surprise searches of inmates and their living, working, education, and recreation areas are essential. Oak Park Heights staff have practiced and performed their mission to perfection. Although weapons do appear from time to time—as with the football-game stabbing—it is the exception rather than the rule.

Numerous local gang members as well as established gang leaders reside in the prison. Yet on a daily basis, gang activity is not a major issue. Organized efforts by leaders to use their power and intimidation is rigorously controlled.

The last question, which is directly connected to the other aspects of a well-run prison, is whether it is safe to walk around the prison. The climate at Oak Park Heights is generally comfortable and friendly. Workers, administrators, community organizations, professional groups, college classes, and the general public have toured and walked through virtually every area of the prison without discomfort or alarm. Although the potential for disruption always exists, Oak Park Heights is one of the safest prisons ever built.

◆ ◆ ◆

This environment wasn't created by luck or accident. It began in 1982 with the prison's opening under the leadership of Warden Frank Wood. He established the underlying philosophy of how this prison was going to operate—and not just for those who worked and lived at the facility, but for those in the community who would someday face the offenders when they were released.

Wood was the best prison administrator and warden I have known. He could have become the successful CEO of any corporation or, without even knowing the intricate details of the game of football, been a winning coach. He would analyze and study any situation, prepare for any event, leave no detail unattended, and find a way to win. I know I wouldn't have bet against him. He operated a prison that way, and it has paid the state dividends for years.

Recognizing Minnesota would need such a prison in its future, Wood spent years conceiving this unique facility. He was integral in every aspect of the planning, organization, and design. Yet his most significant contributions came in overseeing the operational aspects of the prison. As he stated, "Prisons do not run safely by accident, they run safely by design." Oak Park Heights became world famous for its design. The philosophy, foundation, and preparation for that blueprint was put in place and then carefully executed and monitored by Wood. In 1992, he was promoted to Deputy Commissioner of Institutions and put his imprint on all Minnesota prisons. This imprint remains and is a model throughout the nation and world.

Through the years, Oak Park Heights has provided an opportunity for inmates to change the behavior that got them there. Wood's articulated goal was to create an environment conducive to rehabilitation for those offenders who are inclined to want to make a change in their lives. This fundamental concept underlies incentive-based programming, where bad behavior brings consequences and good behavior brings rewards. For all inmates, Oak Park Heights offers a fresh start, an opportunity to live a different way predicated on their behavior.

Yet it is important not to confuse dignity, respect, programming, and decency with weakness and loss of control. Inmates do not control anything inside the walls. Everything is structured in accordance with strict policy and procedure. This harmonizes in creating a safe, secure, and humane environment for inmates and staff.

It can't be forgotten that despite all of the positive elements, Oak Park Heights is still a prison. It's not a playground or a summer camp. It's not a place where complacency can exist or a place for officers who are not committed to their work. People get hurt if policy and procedure aren't carefully followed. In prison—especially one housing high-risk inmates—there will always be problems. Running a prison takes constant review and fine tinkering. It requires professional staff at all levels that are serious about their work and, most of all, believe in the philosophy that supports them.

Ninety-five percent of the inmates here have committed a physical act of violence against their victims. More than fifty percent killed someone. A quarter or more are first degree murderers, and a significant number are serving life without parole. This is a distilled population of the very worse offenders who have ended up at the end of the line. They have committed despicable acts against society, been a major management problem at another institution, or both. Yet how they are treated and managed sets the tone for the environment that exists. States and countries that operate prisons where violence is present every day and the mood is volatile don't have worse inmates, they just manage them poorly.

Playing
the Game

From my first day in a supermax prison, I knew this was not going to be easy. I was walking down a corridor when I observed four inmates pointing at me from the other side of the staff dining area. These inmates were all in the Big House for murder, and they had the tough look of men who had spent much of their life in prison—tattoos decorating their forearms, beefed-up bodies from too much time with barbells, and hard expressions on their faces. As they pointed at me, they talked quietly among themselves, staring me down. They were playing the game, cold-blooded killers trying to threaten me. Their intimidation was working, but I could never let them know it.

The game had begun, and I was one of the players.

I started in the corrections business when I was just twenty-one years old. After graduating from the University of Minnesota with a bachelor of science degree in education, my first job was at Minnesota's Ramsey County juvenile Woodview Detention Home. I didn't know much about offenders, but I quickly learned. Through the ensuing years, I worked as a juvenile and, later, adult probation officer, became superintendent of Ramsey County's Correctional Facility, and served on the state parole board. On June 30, 1982, I left my job as parole board vice chairman and on July 1, 1982, began working in Minnesota's new supermax prison at Oak Park Heights as Internal Affairs Investigator. In 1996, when Frank Wood retired as the state's Commissioner of Corrections, I left my post as his deputy to become Oak Park Heights warden.

Going to work each day in a supermax prison was different from anything I had previously experienced. It was tough for me at first. I had always been confident of my surroundings and sure of my work responsibilities. My new workplace, however, was extraordinary.

Nothing was as it seemed. The inmates existed in a society where they fought against each and every rule with cunning and wiles, or simple brute physical force if need be. The aura of violence, the cons, the hidden agendas, the deceits, and the intimidations—it was all part of playing the game.

Warden Jim Bruton surrounded by the prison's perimeter of cyclone fencing, barbed wire, and razor ribbon. (Photograph © Layne Kennedy)

In my previous job assignments, I had become acquainted with numerous offenders and was one of the reasons many of these inmates were in prison in the first place. As a state parole board member, I sat at their parole hearings, turned down their parole requests, and held their fates in my hands, determining how much of their sentences they would serve. For many, it was several decades—if not their whole lives—and they didn't look kindly on me.

Inmate Allan Mariano was one. He was a long-term felon who had been convicted of butchering his family. I first came face to face with him sitting across a table at his parole hearing as I reviewed his case. He was a plain person, indistinguishable from anyone you'd pass on the street. Yet he watched me that whole hearing, his cold eyes never leaving my face. At the hearing's conclusion, Mariano was told he would be doing every single day of his twenty-year sentence. I looked him directly in the eye and said that given his history and these gruesome murders, he would never have the opportunity for parole. He presented too much of a risk to public safety.

I shuddered when I passed this judgment. Twenty years was too long for me to realistically comprehend—two decades out of a lifetime locked away without a taste of freedom. Yet Mariano seemed unperturbed, and his response sent a chill down my spine. He stared back at me and didn't blink as he replied, "Twenty years . . . that's not that far away."

I was never sure if his response was simply calm and cool nonchalance, or if it was a threat—"Just wait: When I get out in twenty years, I'm coming for your blood."

I certainly was not about to ask him.

Mariano was at Oak Park Heights when I began work. I don't know if he remembered what he said at the hearing a few years before, but I certainly did. Mariano's case and numerous others like it were the source for some of my discomfort at my new job.

Inmate Howard Melton was another. Melton was a classic felon who lived a life devoted to lawlessness. Yet the first time I met him, I felt empathy for him. It's a good thing, too, as our careers—his of crime, mine of corrections—were intertwined for more than thirty years in the system.

I first met Melton when he was ten years old. When I began my career at Woodview Detention Home, I used to lock the cell door behind him and wish him "Good night." I frequently tucked him in for the night, as he was charged to the center continuously, usually for non-violent crimes.

I never felt Melton was dangerous, just a crook. He always had a smile on his face and a sense of humor. Being locked away from his home never seemed to bother him. It also didn't seem to bother him that he lacked a sense of right or wrong when it came to taking items that didn't belong to him.

After I moved to juvenile probation, Melton and I soon became reacquainted: I was now his probation officer. I dealt with school issues and theft problems throughout his years in the juvenile system. Melton came from a pretty good home, and I got to know his parents well. They were nice people, but didn't have a clue how to control their son.

Five years later, I transferred to adult probation and Melton graduated to adult court. It wasn't long before he was on probation to me again, now as an adult offender. Nothing much had changed for Melton; he had only grown older. The smile was bigger, his charisma even stronger, and he was now a better thief as well.

After I joined the state parole board, I was soon sitting across the table from Melton during a parole hearing. He had now hit the big time by ending up in prison. He still had his smile, even from inside the prison walls. It didn't look like he was ever going to change.

When I came to Oak Park Heights, there was Melton again. Here he was in a supermax prison, yet the smile lit up the first time he spotted me in this new setting. He acted as if we were long-lost relatives, reunited at last.

Inmate Herbert Cummings and I had also risen through the prison system together. But whereas Melton had some warmth to his soul, Cummings was pure hatred. He had spent his life in and out of institutions, always making his stays miserable for everyone who knew him.

I had heard about Cummings long before I ever met him. His mean disposition was legend among officers, yet I thought most of it had to be made up or at least embellished. I was wrong. He wasn't nearly as bad as everyone said. He was worse.

I first met him when I was the Ramsey County Correctional Facility superintendent. I was walking by his cell and said, "Good morning." Cummings replied, "Fuck you!"

It was the start of a relationship that never got any better.

Cummings found ingenious ways to get in trouble. One of his favorite schemes was to take a job as a room attendant at a motel. Waiting until a patron left, Cummings used his master key to unlock the door, ordered massive feasts from room service, devoured the meal, and as a result, got fired and sometimes prosecuted.

Cummings was obese and suffered numerous maladies, often with oozing sores plaguing his body. His poor health was attributed to years of living on the streets and poor health practices. He was in constant need of care yet gave the medical staff a rough time. Nothing was ever good enough for him, and he always felt there was a conspiracy against him. He complained to me once that the guards spied on him as he sat on the toilet having bowel movements. I always investigated complaints against staff, but this one I knew wasn't true. Still, Cummings believed it was—all part of a deep-seated paranoia.

On my first day as Oak Park Heights warden, I was in the Segregation Unit only a few moments when I heard a loud hammering on a cell door. Accompanying the banging came a long, bellowing stream of obscenities. I asked one of the officers who was making all the noise. The officer replied, "Oh, that's Cummings." He had been a small-time hood, and I couldn't believe he was now at Oak Park Heights. Convicted of terroristic threats, he had been sentenced to prison, yet because his behavior was so disruptive, he was now at the Big House. I hadn't seen him for several years, so I walked up to his cell and looked in the window. Cummings stopped his yelling and banging, and said to me in a growl, "Bruton, what are you doing here?"

I told him that I was the new warden.

Cummings replied, "Bullshit! You're not the warden here!"

I told him to calm down, then advised him I had just been appointed.

For a moment, we actually started to have a calm conversation as he asked a few more questions. He suddenly stopped his line of talk and said, "No shit, you're really the warden here?" He then burst into one of his obnoxious fits of rage, banging on his door like a wild animal and screaming at me, "Then where the fuck is my toilet paper?"

To be a warden or prison officer, the first trick is to not let inmates intimidate you—or at least, not to show it in any way, shape, or form. There can never be any doubt as to who is in charge of the prison.

Intimidation and fear—it's all many inmates know. Every encounter, every conversation, every walk down a hallway is part of the game of intimidation. They give you a cold stare for long periods of time, daring you to break eye contact. Or conversely, they completely avoid you, pretending you don't exist in their world. Aggression, loud voices, swearing, and invading your personal space are all part of their tactics—if you let them.

I learned this lesson quickly. You cannot become a part of their world and allow the intimidation to begin. But it's not always a game of subtle violence; you can also disarm them with politeness. When the four murderers tried to intimidate me on my first day on the job, I walked directly up to the group and asked if there was something I could help them with. Not expecting this approach, they became embarrassed and the group broke up. The more I walked around the prison and the more contact I had with inmates, the more comfortable I became. This was my job, and I intended to do it responsibly and effectively.

To demonstrate that officers were always in control of every aspect of the prison, I used to walk into the most potentially hostile areas where there were numerous inmates present, such as the corridors, outside yard, or gym. This wasn't intended to be an act of superiority or bravery, but a way of demonstrating this was "our" prison and we would go wherever we wanted to, when we wanted to. Like so many other things that we did as officials, it was a message as part of the game.

Inmate Joseph Daniels was a long-term felon with a grisly history of violence. He had been shuffled between federal prisons due to his ongoing extreme behavior and was now transferred to Oak Park Heights, delivered directly from a Segregation cell at a United States penitentiary. He had seen nothing but isolation for seven years and had refused to converse with a prison officer in all that time. He was not a nice person. Daniels was built like a wrecking ball and had a disposition to match. He was surly and uncommunicative, yet he let it be known that he relished the opportunity for a fresh start in new surroundings. We decided to give him that chance.

Initially, Daniels's adjustment was good. He did what he was told without complaint. Soon he was going to work every day in the industry shops and doing well.

Then I started hearing rumors about his behind the scenes activities. I had no proof, but had been told that he was using what he'd learned as a dangerous convict to muscle, terrorize, and bully. It was a part of who he had become over the years—and he was good at it. Daniels was a monster of a man with massive arms decorated with ferocious tattoos shown off by shirts that he had ripped the sleeves out of. Intimidation was his means of survival.

I decided Daniels needed a little reminder of who was in charge. It was within our authority to transfer Daniels back to the Federal Bureau of Prisons without any explanation; he was only with us because we allowed him to stay.

I knew Daniels well from the short time he had been with us and we got along civilly. I stopped him in the corridor one day and told him I wanted him to listen to what I had to say and not respond. He agreed.

I told him that we had been hearing things about him, and he immediately interrupted to explain his side. I reminded him to listen until I was finished, and he agreed again. I started and was stopped a second time by his defensive interruption. I politely asked him a third time to wait until I was finished before responding.

We started over again and this time he listened.

I said to him, "Look, we are hearing things about you strong-arming other inmates and extorting money from them. We don't know if it's true and have little concern at this time about proving it. All we know for sure is this: If we hear one more negative comment about you from any of our sources, this is what is going to occur. You will be awakened the next morning at 5 A.M. You will be asked to pack your belongings and will be escorted upstairs to the holding room to await transfer back to the federal system. And you know where you will go from there—right back to a Segregation cell. Do you understand?"

"I understand," he said quietly.

Daniels never caused a problem again and stayed to the end of his sentence several years later. He just needed a reminder about the rules of the game.

Sometimes the game takes on all the appearances of chess. There were feints and attacks and diversions, setups and phony routines and carefully laid out schemes that kept me and my officers always on our toes.

One afternoon, I walked into a housing unit and immediately an inmate came up to talk to me. This wasn't necessarily unusual, but it could have been an attempt to distract me from something else. Inmates frequently came to talk to me, but his hurried manner was suspicious.

I looked around and noticed a second inmate casually standing at the top of the stairs leading to an upper tier of cells. This was also not unusual. However, my first thought was that he was a lookout, watching over the unit to be sure that no staff entered an area so as to protect drug or sexual activity, illicit tattooing, gambling, an assault, the hiding of weapons, or some other illegal goings on.

I immediately told the inmate who approached me that I would talk to him later and climbed up to the inmate on the steps. I figured if he moved quickly in retreat, he was going to warn someone.

He didn't move, so initially I thought my suspicions were unfounded. However, it could have been set up for me to think exactly that and respond the way I did. Maybe the real activity, with another lookout stationed elsewhere, was at the other end of the cellblock.

Each of these inmates was positioned like a piece in a real-life chess game, guarding their king from danger. I had broken up this play—but I never found out exactly what I had halted.

I prided myself on having a pretty good handle on what was occurring inside the prison, but deep down I always knew there was a lot that we didn't know. As the saying goes, "You don't know what you don't know," and it's important to always recognize that fact. I wasn't so presumptuous as to think I knew what all the inmates were up to at a given time. Sometimes, I remembered back to fishing as a kid and wishing that all the water surrounding my boat would disappear so I could see just for an instant what fish might be swimming there. As warden, I often wondered what was really going on deep within the prison. What were the inmates doing that we didn't know about? What escape plan or assault were they plotting?

It was often difficult to turn off all this cloak and dagger paranoia when I walked out the front door at the end of a long day and entered the free world.

There is a cardinal rule in running a prison—no unnecessary surprises. It is never in the facility's best interest to surprise a population of dangerous felons. These people are used to settling their problems with violence, and thus everything must be kept under consistent control. When a surprise is sprung on inmates, you never know what might happen.

Another cardinal rule in prisons is to never give bad news to inmates when they are not secured in their cells, and never give it on a Friday or a weekend. The reasoning behind the Friday and weekend rule is simple: Don't give bad news on these days unless you want to work through the weekend to control an incident or riot when fewer staff are on duty.

Several years ago, the Minnesota Department of Corrections' prisons were severely overcrowded. As a result, we began to rent cells in county jails to house prisoners. For the most part, this worked well. In one of the jails, however, these cardinal rules were not understood.

It was a Saturday morning and many of the inmates were out of their cells and in the main part of the cellblock. For whatever reason, the staff decided it was a good time to notify the inmates of some significant changes that required more lock-in time and less programming. If someone had asked me what I thought the response would be to this announcement at this particular time with the inmates out of their cells, I would have warned, "They are going to tear your jail apart." And they did. The message given by the jail was legitimate. It was just given at the exact wrong time.

A good time to deliver a message is at 10 P.M. when the inmates are all secured in their cells. This will give officers many hours to assess the prisoners' reactions before cells are opened in the morning. You have to do what you have to do, but the timing is critical to maintaining control. Simply put, it is essential to stay one move ahead in the game.

To keep in control, we also had to keep our word. We had to stick to our own rules religiously, whether they were key, life-threatening regulations or minor ones. Changing the food menu without notice is a minor transgression, but it is a foolish mistake to make and can result in the loss of good faith. If the menu called for hamburgers and French fries—a popular meal in prisons—then hamburgers and French fries it better be. Making a last-minute switch to peanut butter-and-jelly sandwiches is a sure recipe for trouble. There is no reason to put the staff in a position to be hurt, have the prison damaged, or lose control over so insignificant an issue.

There are acceptable surprises that the inmate population learns to deal with on a regular basis. These are the surprises that directly connect to security—surprise searches, unit shakedowns, preventative lockups, and so forth. There can be no warning for these, and although unpopular, in most respects inmates accept them—albeit grudgingly.

It's essential in a supermax prison to have proactive preventative lockups and searches. These searches sometimes can take as long as a week to complete. At Oak Park Heights, the inmates were usually notified while locked in their cells that the unit was on immediate lockup status. Several cells were quickly entered as shakedowns of certain suspicious prisoners' living quarters were made. A memorandum outlining exactly what was going to occur was then delivered to all of the other inmates so they knew what was happening over the next few days.

Subtle messages are often sent back and forth between the inmate population and the prison administration. At Oak Park Heights, the preventative surprise lockups have been a practice since the prison's opening. The inmates expect it, even though they never know when it might occur. Sometimes, however, they try to get control of the decision-making by forcing the lockup so they can have it when they want it. Simply put, it's a power play on their part.

One day, a small screwdriver was missing from the industry shop. A missing tool is a major issue in a supermax prison: It could become a murder weapon or aid in an escape. We had to make every effort to locate the screwdriver as soon as possible, including locking up the unit in the process, if necessary.

The tool was not located, and the unit was locked up. For one full week, officers searched every inch of the industry area, the unit, and the cells. We didn't find it.

At some point, if the search is unsuccessful, a decision has to be made to re-open the unit and get the inmates back to work. I reluctantly made the decision. I believed the tool had been disposed of—flushed down a toilet or somehow destroyed. The unit was re-opened.

A few minutes after the inmates were back at work in the industry shop, the missing screwdriver reappeared, sitting innocently on a chair. Why? A message was being sent: "We will decide when lockups occur."

The inmates estimated it was about time for a surprise lockup, and they wanted to show their power by setting the date and time; they knew a missing tool would initiate it. They took control for a short time, forced the lockup, and by returning the tool, told us what they did.

The inmates figured it would be several months now before the next lockup, giving them some breathing room for whatever plans they might be hatching—escape plots, drug deals, and so on. But just weeks later, I ordered a proactive surprise lockup. The inmates were stunned; they had just come off their forced week-long lockup and weren't expecting this. Our message back to them was clear: "We make the decisions around here."

Sometimes, training requirements, holidays, or other prison activities required inmates to be locked in their cells for long periods of time. When their behavior was good and the action routine, I tried to send a message to them in appreciation—a snack of a candy bar or ice cream delivered to their cells in the afternoon. The public may not appreciate giving inmates treats for any reason, yet it was important to the running of the prison. The inmates appreciated it, and it was so little to give for so much in return, a subtle message going a long way toward operating a humane environment.

This game never comes to an end. The opponent's move may be spontaneous or it may be a strategy years in the planning. Against such opposition, staying a move ahead is not an easy task.

One move I made might appear minor, but probably was significant enough to make Oak Park Heights a safer institution for the future.

We had been having too much noise and one fight too many in the corridors. The prison corridors have to be reasonably quiet in order to hear radio communications and assess the daily mood of the prison environment. Fights always occur in prisons—at Oak Park Heights, almost every prisoner has a violent history. But fights involving large numbers of inmates in the corridors can't be tolerated. The next step is a riot.

Inmates were warned many times about yelling in the corridors. Some had their movement time suspended. But this strategy was not working—the noise level was still too high.

Finally, a large fight broke out one afternoon between several inmates. After the fight was halted, I issued a new order: No more than seven inmates could be free in the corridors at one time. The rule was exhaustive to enforce, but it made for a safer and quieter environment. It was a step to stay one move ahead, and had a lasting effect on the safety of staff and other inmates.

There are other moves we make behind the scenes—secret moves the inmates may never learn of—designed to pre-empt their game. Escapes are always a concern in supermax prisons. A primary responsibility of a prison is to protect the public. When taxpayers spend millions of dollars to build such facilities and millions more to operate them, they expect that inmates sentenced to live there, stay there.

There has never been an escape from Oak Park Heights or, as far as I was aware, even an attempted escape. With the most high-risk and incorrigible offenders housed there, it is unusual to boast such a record. Yet the preventative practices in place have been a strong anticipatory type of management through the last two decades. The element of surprise and avoidance of routine have kept the inmates off guard and unable to do long-range planning for escapes.

When I took over at Oak Park Heights, one of my first directives to my administrative staff was to form individual teams involving staff from all levels of the organization. Their mission was to find an escape route out of prison by any means. Working out these possible escapes, we learned a great deal about the prison, uncovering several construction flaws and vulnerable areas. I slept better at night when we finished.

Over the years, we used other exercises to test different areas of the prison's security and resolve. Each test helped us to maintain the edge and to understand our opponents, preparing us for their every move and keeping us in control.

The game continues throughout the day and in the dark of night, on weekends and on holidays, during the Super Bowl and the World Series, whether we're awake or asleep. It's played every minute without rest. It is us against them, and we'd better hope we are always one move ahead. It's a tough game, played for keeps, with no holds barred.

I received a phone call early in my career; the speaker on the other end didn't identify himself, only said, "You're going to be shot when you leave today."

As I left work that evening and walked to my car, I tried my best to keep my cool and not be intimidated. No shots were fired, and I breathed a big sigh of relief.

I never found out who the caller was—perhaps a felon, perhaps a joker—but I still remember that voice and those words.

Doing Time

The key to surviving in prison comes down to one thing—respect. If you don't win the respect of other inmates, your time will be spent in hell. And if you don't in turn respect others—especially the cons demanding that respect—you might never see the end of your sentence.

Respect is central to inmate culture, yet it is a different type of respect than we practice outside in the free world. Treating each other in a dignified and honorable manner is for the most part important to all of us. But among murders and sex offenders respect means something different. In prison, respect can be a matter of life or death.

More prison fights, assaults, and murders have probably been committed because one con disrespected another than for any other motive. Here, respect may mean stepping aside for another con in the corridor or letting someone ahead of you in the meal line. It may also be a demand to subject yourself to another con's orders—whatever they may be. Disrespect may be looking at someone wrong, talking about someone behind their back, not paying a debt, cheating at cards, or a variety of other acts. Disrespect can make you a marked man—and you'll never know when the retribution will come.

There is a strict hierarchy among cons that demands respect. A con's place in this hierarchy comes from the crime committed. At the top of the scale are those who have killed a law enforcement officer. Among fellow cons, these criminals are believed to have performed an honorable act and made the world a better place. To rid society of someone whose job is "To Protect and Serve" is an example of doing right. It's a perverse viewpoint—especially to correctional officers whose job it is to guard these cons at the top of the inmate hierarchy.

Next down on the hierarchy are the lifers—cons serving life sentences for first degree murder. In addition, the more years of their sentences they have served, the higher the regard from fellow cons. Those that have done many years in prison and met the challenge to become comfortable in their surrounding are the true "convicts," a term of pride to many. They are warriors and survivors who become institutionalized and live in prison every day like most of us do in the free world. These lifers are seasoned veterans in the prison world, and they are looked up to and mostly left alone. There's one key reason for this: They have nothing left to lose.

Cons who committed a violent act with a gun, such as an armed robbery, are next on the scale. Using a weapon to obtain money is a quality demanding respect in this neighborhood.

A serial killer, although terrifying in the eyes of the public, doesn't automatically earn respect or carry his fearsome reputation into prison. I have seen some serial killers who brutally murdered many people, yet were in constant danger from other cons because they were weak and frightened no one in prison. They had been vicious to a helpless or vulnerable victim, but in these surroundings, the tables are often turned and they're the victims. Serial killers do not earn a reputable status in prison by their body count alone. And often they are viewed as simply insane, which places them outside the respect hierarchy as simply someone to stay away from or ignore.

At the bottom of the hierarchy are those cons doing time for sex crimes. These cons are blatantly disregarded as scum by most other inmates who view sexual offenses as an aberration from what is acceptable criminal conduct. It may seem ironic, but it's a commonly held belief.

High-profile sexual assault cases that garner lots of media attention often attach a bull's-eye to the back of the perpetrators of such deplorable acts. When they arrive in prison, these offenders are in immediate life-threatening danger. I recall some years back when a horrifying case received a great deal of media attention. The offender kidnapped, raped, and murdered a young waitress on St. Paul's west side. Shortly after the offender entered Oak Park Heights, he was stabbed in the face, a needle-sharp laundry pin driven up his nose as retaliation for his despicable crime. The con delivering the payback was a double murderer, but in his mind there was no similarity between the crimes.

The lowest of the low in the prison hierarchy are child molesters. Other cons call them "low life" or "baby rapers" to their faces and will tell them flat out that they're "sick motherfuckers." I've heard it all.

It's tough to keep child molesters safe from other offenders who deplore their acts against a child. Some inmates think of their own children and the rage they would feel if their loved ones were the victims. In the early 1980s, an inmate was stabbed to death in the corridor at Stillwater prison. The assailant later admitted his motivation for the killing was simply because the victim was a child molester and "needed to be killed." The "prison justice" logic might not make sense outside, but I sometimes wonder how much really does in this strange world inside the walls.

When the crime committed is not a factor in earning respect, the conduct of the offender is paramount. There is great respect for and distance kept from those who are physically large and think nothing of using their brawn to get their way. There are others who survive because they let it be known early on in their confinement that they are not afraid to go to war if necessary. Sometimes it takes aggressive behavior to get the message across to the predators.

The other type of offenders who are generally left alone are those that are clearly recognized as mentally ill. If a con gets a reputation for being sick or insane, he is for the most part not preyed upon because others are never quite sure what he might do. He may attack someone twice his size or go after anyone at any time. The mentally ill inmates are wild cards, and most cons simply choose not to mess with them.

Adjustment to the bizarre environment of prison doesn't come easy. The inside is filled with unusual activity, from running inmate "stores" to clandestine tattoo "parlors" to gambling rackets, and unusual people, from drug dealers to sexual predators.

Most prisons have a secret and illegal inmate store run by a special type of offender. These cons gather supplies and food, buying and bartering from other inmates, and stockpiling items in their cells or other locations. Their stores sell just about anything cons need; the most common items are snack foods—potato chips, cupcakes, soda pop, and cookies. This food is in demand because inmates are not allowed unlimited access to the legal prison canteen; they are scheduled to go only at certain times. Or they may have run out of money and want something immediately and on credit. The store operator might hide his wares in clothing, shoes, behind books, in the unit washing machines or dryers, secured under tables, or beneath pillows, blankets, and mattresses. Random surprise cell searches usually uncover the store stock and catch the culprit, but he is often back in business as soon as the search is over. It takes a special type of con to run such a store—a scheming and conniving expert that understands the unique aspects of supply and demand within prison.

Other inmates offer drugs and shanks for sale. These are truly black marketeers running undercover lucrative businesses. Keeping these items safely hidden is obviously essential, and a crafty con may hide them in a variety of places. Some inmates painstakingly drill holes into their shoe heels or soles, or sew secret pockets or knife sheaths into their clothing. They might cut out portions of book pages as clandestine compartments to store a marijuana stash or slide a shank down the binding of a Bible. Hypodermic needles can be stuffed into the putty surrounding a cell window. Knives might be attached to a string and hung behind sinks or lowered down the plumbing of a toilet. The mechanical interior workings of machines in the Industry programs or everyday items such as washers and dryers, irons, TVs, radios, and other electronic equipment all make ideal hiding spots; electronic items can only be purchased by inmates from certain approved vendors and even then, everything is carefully taken apart and checked by officers before it's passed to the inmates. Contraband is also commonly hidden in toothpaste tubes or toilet paper rolls, inside watches, in bags of snack food, or inside a simple ballpoint pen. Within a prison classroom—which is similar to any school classroom—every single item is fair game as a hiding place. We once found a bag of tobacco on top of the security-room's bubble-shaped window that jutted out into a hall.

During a spot search, cons might stuff things into their mouths for a quick, temporary hiding place. I recall an officer took a large shank from an inmate who had it in the small of his back as he tried to get through a search. The groin area, the hair, and under the arms are all common hiding places. The extreme is for a con to swallow an item in a plastic bag or balloon, store it in his stomach, and then vomit it back up or pass it through his digestive system. Others secret items inside their rectums.

The inmates carefully watch the guards and know from experience who will do a full search and who will not—who will just do a pat search and prudishly only go close to the groin and buttocks compared to those guards who will look in their mouths and have the inmate spread their butt cheeks for a thorough search. Inmates are also ingenious at moving items around during a search, sometimes with several inmates involved in the transfers. Cons know more about the officers than the officers sometimes know about each other—or even themselves.

Weapons are made in prison with mind-boggling imagination. A scrap of metal, a piece of hard plastic, a chair leg, a broken wastebasket, a sliver of wood— all are raw material for prisoners to form into dangerous weapons. Pencils or toothbrushes rubbed to razor-sharp points become stilettos. Plastic and wood are ideal materials because they won't be picked up by a metal detector. Small objects are coveted as they can be easily hidden in the mouth to be carried about within prison.

It's an art, and inmates are master artists.

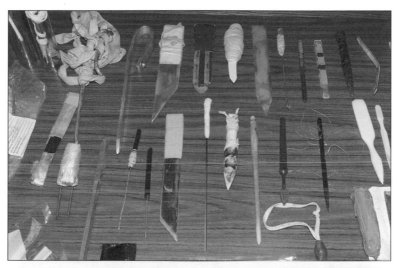

Confiscated shanks, knives, and other weapons.

Inmates have made serious assaults on one another with just a bar of soap held in a sock and swung with powerful—and potentially deadly—force.

Ingenuity is the key ingredient. Revenge the mother of invention.

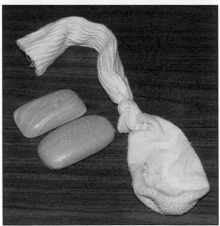

Drugs get smuggled into prison by some of the most despicable methods. In the visiting area, visitors might hide the drugs anywhere from personal undergarments to baby diapers. Often, the drugs are concealed in a balloon, and during a hug or kiss, the visitor transfers the stash to the inmate, who swallows the balloon whole. The inmate "stores" it in his stomach, and then vomits it back up or passes it through his digestive system. Others hide items inside their own rectums.

It sounds crude, but it's the reality of prison.

Confiscated drugs and drug paraphernalia.

A stash of marijuana hidden in a hollowed-out bar of Dial soup.

Inmates make tattoo guns with creative flare. A gun can be built with a guitar string as the needle mounted in a ballpoint pen shaft with a bit of rubber, masking tape, and a toothbrush to link the needle to a motor. These motors are taken from electric razors or audio equipment. When using an audio component, the volume control dictates the speed of the needle's vibration.

Prison-made tattoo gun discovered hidden in deodorant container.

Another undercover business in prisons is tattoo parlors. Tattoo artists usually learn their trade outside. Inside, they are highly respected because of their creative skills and are much sought after by inmate customers.

Tats are hot items in prison. They can be status symbols or simply inmate art. Some cons use them for personal symbolism, depicting the names or images of loved ones. Popular prison art includes a spider tattooed on a con's elbow, a symbol conveying confinement. Others have a teardrop inked below an eye, giving them the appearance of permanently crying. Some tats warn fellow cons that respect is due with a subtle message saying "Don't mess with me." Many inmates desire the tattoos as a display of their convict status, the illegal tats providing proof of their prison experiences and a showcase of the time they've done. Tats might identify a con's previous criminal activity, such as performing a prison murder.

Certain tattoos are known as "brands" and signify belonging to prison gangs, a message instilling fear in others to steer clear. Some get inscribed with white-supremacist logos like those of the Aryan Brotherhood, or AB monogram. To hide the Aryan Brotherhood affiliation from watchful guards but still identify themselves to fellow cons, they might use tattooed nicknames such as Alice Baker, or simply Alice, or The Brand.

Upon admitting new offenders, most prisons take photos to document all of their tattoos to be stored in their files. This allows for easy identification of any new tattoos, which would be a violation of prison rules and subject to discipline. Prisons attempt to combat tattooing for health reasons. Poor hygiene due to overused and dirty tattooing needles and insufficient cleanliness create a significant health hazard. This forces tattooers to make their shops secretive and mobile.

These entrepreneurs make tattoo guns in all sorts of creative fashion. A gun can be built using a thin guitar string as the needle that is mounted in a plastic ballpoint pen shaft with a rubber band or Pink Pearl eraser, masking tape, and a toothbrush to link the needle to a motor. These motors are taken from electric razors, cassette-tape recorders, or CD players. Power comes from either batteries or an AC/DC adaptor plugged into a socket. When using an audio component, the volume control dictates the speed of the needle's vibration. Tattoo artists sometime obtain supplies by stealing permanent ink from hobby craft class or the education area. Whatever it takes.

Guards generally know which inmates are the tattooers, making these artists' work tedious and time consuming as they require equally creative methods to keep staff from interfering. A lookout is essential to operating a parlor. An inmate skilled as an observer and detractor watches for any corrections officers. A signal—whether it's a noise or movement—alerts the cell serving as the parlor to stop the artwork and hide all tools.

To keep their businesses alive, tattoo artists must also be artists at ingeniously hiding their equipment from the watchful eyes of suspecting corrections officers. They break down their guns back into innocent-looking pens and audio players or stash the components inside shampoo bottles, stuff them deep within bars of soap or items of food, or temporarily hide them in their clothing. As good as the hiding place may be, a seasoned correctional officer has found items there before and likely will find them again. Still, inmates have the time and will to always be dreaming up new and better hiding places to keep their contraband safe, at least for a short period of time. Gambling is a big time operation in prison. Cons run numbers rackets, point-spread boards, and betting pools on all sort of games. During inmates' free time, card, checkers, and chess games are common sights—and there's usually something at stake. Toothpicks are often used for poker chips, although inmates will never admit to their worth.

One afternoon I walked into a cellblock and spotted several inmates that I knew well sitting at a table playing cards. Toothpicks were laying all over the table in neat stacks as well as in an ante pile. I approached them and with a tongue-in-cheek smile on my face said, "Now you guys wouldn't be gambling back here would you?" They smiled back and one responded, "Warden, we would never do anything like that—there are rules against that! We're only playing for toothpicks." Deep down I was wondering what each one of those toothpicks was worth.

Games and gambling might be great fun for cons and a way to do the time, but these are rarely just friendly games. An inmate better pay up any money owed or he may pay with his life. All too often after a prison assault, I feared that the victim had been the recipient of a ghastly beating simply due to bad debts.

Prison sex is one of the most mysterious areas of prison culture. Without question, sexual activity exists in prisons, although I believe the level is significantly diminished in the Minnesota prison system primarily due to the guards' awareness and constant effort to combat it whenever possible.

When I became warden, we were having an unusually high number of incidents of inmates masturbating in view of female officers. Inmates would wait for a female officer to enter the unit or until she passed by their cells during routine room checks, and then expose themselves to the officer. It was disturbing to staff, and it became clear that the rule violation and penalty for the act didn't outweigh the inmate satisfaction.

Because of this, we made a policy change that significantly decreased these incidents. Following one of these exposures, we immediately hauled the inmate off to the Segregation Unit. If already housed in Segregation, the inmate was moved to a modified cell, and, if in a modified cell, privileges were taken away. This swift change of status deterred offenders with the unpleasant results of their conduct.

Private masturbation is common in prisons—it always has been and always will be. All types of pornographic magazines were outlawed from Minnesota correctional facilities in 2001, hampering the impetus for masturbation somewhat, but inmate imagination still and probably will always provide motivation. Staff runs into this often, and it is difficult to work around, especially for female officers. Unfortunately, it's part of the prison world.

Sex between inmates is also part of the environment. Sometimes, these are consensual relationships; too often, they're prison rapes. As a warden, I can only guess about the frequency of prison sex as it's usually hidden and rarely uncovered.

It's also rare that prison-rape victims come forward to testify against their attackers. Being the victim of a prison rape is one thing, but having your life taken for snitching is another. Still, I am aware of a surprising number of victims of sexual attacks who reported the assault. Usually, they began the sexual activity as voluntary participants, but then the consensual behavior went too far and they ultimately became forced victims. It's another of the pitfalls and grim realities of doing time.

There are always some cons who are sexual predators. I've seen some offenders who would think nothing of sexually attacking a young, vulnerable inmate in prison, but then abhor a child molester for his crimes on the outside. It's an ironic double standard as to what is acceptable behavior, but that's part of the inmate mindset.

It's a sad fact of the prison world, but only the strong survive. Weaker offenders often have to pay others for their safety, either for protection or simply to not be beaten up. They may have to perform unpleasant cleaning tasks, give up desserts, buy from the inmate store and give their purchases to someone else as bribes. They might constantly have to ask family and friends to send them money which in turn becomes extortion pay for their safety. Or it might be for a sexual transaction.

The underworld of activity is endless. For a warden or guard to be on top of everything is virtually impossible. The scheming, the strong-arming, the bartering, the passing of items from cell to cell, the smuggling, lying, cheating, extortion—it never ends.

Some offenders are just not capable of handling the pressure. At times, they decide to escape by suicide. Killing yourself in prison is not easy as inmates lack the tools to do it cleanly or with finesse. When a suicide is successful, it's often a gruesome scene that has been carefully planned out. Most prison suicides are from hanging, wrist cutting with a homemade shank, or an overdose of pills.

I was fortunate: During my tenure of managing institutions, no inmate committed suicide. Part of this was pure luck. I saw several serious attempts and some, although horrible and bloody, were pure attention-seeking behavior.

When we became aware that an inmate was capable of suicide, we usually placed him in an area where he could be continually monitored by video and audio, and guards could check on him frequently. The inmate was stripped of his clothing and everything in his cell that could be used to harm himself. We couldn't even leave him with his underwear as he might tear them up and hang himself. The inmate was then placed in a suicide gown, commonly known as the Banana Suit,

Yellow Suit, or simply, the Dress. This piece of clothing is made out of Kevlar with straps in the back that hold the gown on with heavy-duty Velcro. The outfit looks like a thick life jacket and is similar in appearance to a hospital gown without sleeves. Like a strait jacket, it is well designed to prevent tearing or cutting so the potential suicide can't harm himself. Although not a garment to wear to a style show, the Dress serves its purpose well.

The Dress won't win any fashion shows, but it serves its purpose well. Like a strait jacket, it's well designed for its purpose—to prevent a potential suicide from harming himself.

When we became aware that an inmate was capable of suicide, we stripped him of his clothing and everything in his cell that could be used to harm himself. We couldn't even leave him with his underwear as he might tear them up and hang himself.

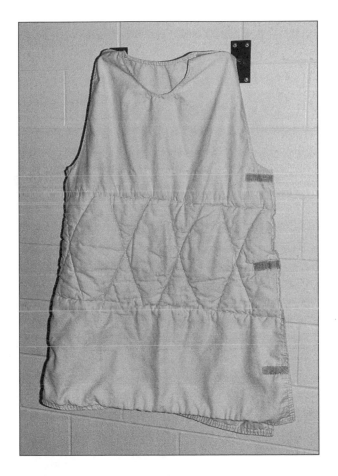

The inmate was then placed in this suicide gown—commonly known as the Banana Suit, Yellow Suit, or simply, the Dress.

Restraining a berserk inmate is a job for the prison's Security Squad. The team dons its full riot gear. A canister of mixed tear and pepper gas is then shot into the cell through the food pass. If the inmate remains uncooperative and continues to refuse directives, the squad rushes the inmate. A full–body plexiglass shield is used to bulldoze the inmate into a corner of his cell where he can be subdued.

It's not a pretty scene, but it's all too often a necessary one.

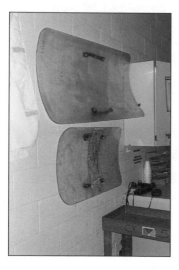

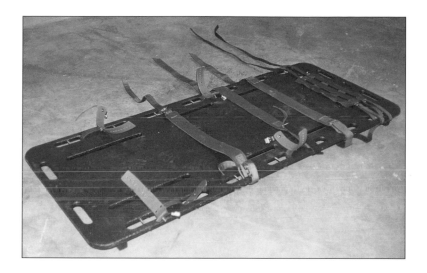

The full-restraint board is used to physically restrain inmates for a period of
time to get them back under control.

An inmate might be attempting to inflict
bodily harm on himself or another con.
Or he might have broken a window,
flooded his cell, or damaged his cell in
some other way.

To protect ourselves, we created new equipment and policies as we learned from experience, which all too often followed a serious assault or injury. Yet some of the planning and preparation that goes into an attack on a guard is so carefully and cruelly premeditated that anticipatory prevention is almost impossible. For example, we devised a restraining helmet after an inmate viciously head-butted an officer in the face. A spit mask became inevitable after another sickening incident. After a further staff assault, we installed a heavy open-top U-bolt in a cement table so inmates could be secured with metal handcuffs while awaiting an examination or being detained during a cell search.

Another reactive policy came after several incidents in the Segregation Unit. Inmates were filling empty milk cartons with their urine and feces and throwing the human waste at officers. I recall well the specific incident that initiated the new procedure. An inmate was serving disciplinary Segregation sentences so he was required to eat in his cell, and an officer went to deliver his meal. The officer was aware that the inmate was prone to lash out in any way possible, so he was especially cautious in opening the door's food pass to deliver the tray. He looked first through the door window; there was the inmate, asleep on his bed covered by a blanket. The officer then carefully opened the chest-level hatch to set the tray into the cell on a cement shelf. As he looked in the window, the inmate sprung like a coiled snake from where he was crouched below the door window—the blanket covered nothing but a dummy made of his extra clothes. The inmate jumped up and threw the carton full of urine and feces into the officer's face.

After this assault, we initiated two things that have diminished the potential for future onslaughts of this nature. At our prompting, the Minnesota Legislature made this act a felony assault to be prosecuted in court. Although this state statute is significant, the real deterrent came with a new procedure. Before a meal is delivered to his cell in the Segregation Unit, an inmate must be sitting or laying on his bed with his hands and feet in full view of the officer. If he is not in compliance with the directive, the meal is not delivered. If he is not in compliance for the next meal, it too is not delivered. For the third meal, the inmate is removed from the cell in full restraints and then placed back in the cell after the meal tray has been left on the cement shelf. This policy works and it works well. I can't recall an offender making it to the third meal without compliance.

To protect officers from attack while escorting the most dangerous and violent inmates, we created another type of prison garb, the full-restraint equipment. This unique wardrobe included the helmet incorporated after the head-butting incident. This soft-shelled helmet has a strap securing it around the inmate's neck and looks much like a football helmet.

Under the helmet, the offender wears the spit mask, which is placed over the head and ties around the shoulders. The mask allows the inmate to breathe, but covers his face with a solid piece of cloth over the mouth and nose to prevent him from spitting or excreting bodily fluids from the nose.

Metal handcuffs are then attached to each wrist and secured to a waist chain that is locked to the reinforced belt loops of the inmate's trousers. The apparatus at the waist is then secured by a single handcuff at the end of a vinyl strap attached at the other end by a handcuff to leg irons on the ankles. This strap, called a bull strap, coordinates the restraint of hands, arms, and legs.

This full-restraint equipment is similar to what serial-killer Hannibal Lecter wore in the movie *The Silence of the Lambs*. While it is cumbersome and inhumane looking, it is a necessity.

Getting a berserk inmate into the full-restraint equipment is another problem altogether. The prison's Security Squad cell-entry team first dons its full riot gear—Kevlar vests, helmets, gas masks, protective gloves, and arm and shin pads. A canister of Freeze Plus P gas—a cocktail mixed of tear gas and CS pepper-capiscum gas—is shot into the closed cell through the food pass. If you ever get hit by CS gas, you'll have learned your lesson and will do anything you're told so as not get a dose again. It causes a burning sensation in the eyes, nose, and throat, overwhelming coughing and shortness of breath, loss of circulation to the extremities of the body, and in some cases, dramatic mucus secretion, nausea, and vomiting. While the gas is having its effect, the squad rushes the inmate. They employ a full-body plexiglass shield to bulldoze the inmate into a corner of his cell where he can be subdued. It's not a pretty scene, but it's all too often a necessary one.

The Human Monster

Inmate Richard Samuels stood just five feet six inches tall and weighed a mere 160 pounds, but he was dynamite packed into that small frame.
One day, I watched officers move him between cells. His legs were shackled together for the short trip, which he resisted with every ounce of his being. His long stringy hair hung in his face as he snarled, growled, swore, and screamed. I had never seen anything like it. The sweating, the shaking, the howling—this was Samuels at his best. I actually questioned whether this was a human being.

During my thirty-five years in corrections, I have worked around thousands of inmates. Most don't stay in my memory. They served their sentences with few problems and passed through the prison system and my mind. Some, however, I remember for a lifetime. Their behavior, attitude, crime, a particular incident—any of these can plant an inmate in my mind. One of the most memorable is Samuels, who came to the newly opened Oak Park Heights prison on an interstate transfer in summer 1982. He had originally been sentenced for murder and would stay in prison for the rest of his life due to scores of additional charges brought against him for assaulting officers. He will be etched in my memory forever.

Shortly after his arrival in Oak Park Heights, Samuels went on a rampage. He was intent on taking the new unit apart. He repeatedly promised us he would "bring the prison to its knees."

Samuels spent his entire stay at Oak Park Heights in the Segregation Unit. This secure unit houses the prison's most dangerous, volatile criminals. It's a jail within a jail, known in prison slang with Big House humor as the Hilton.

To reach Segregation, you descend a narrow, well-lit corridor, the stark cement walls lacking any windows or pictures. Outside the walls is earth; there is no escape as one would only dig deeper into the hillside. The long corridor leads to Complex 5, the Control Unit. From here, you step into a small sally port, which is a secure, enclosed portal that provides a barrier between the corridor and main unit. The doors operate on an interlock system—one door cannot open until another is closed.

Finally you enter the Segregation Unit itself. Its fifty-two cells house inmates serving sentences ranging from a few days to many years. The offenses that have landed them in isolation run from a rule violation, such as disrespecting staff, to an extreme offense, such as the murder of another inmate. The inmates here are confined to their cells twenty-three hours a day, with one hour of recreation in an outdoor enclosed cage, where they exercise alone. They are escorted between cell and recreation yard in restraints and under heavy guard. These security measures make Segregation by far the most controlled area of the prison. For short-term residents, this restricted environment is a temporary punishment. For Segregation's long-term inmates, it is the only way to control them.

Some inmates view the intense security as a challenge to overcome, making Segregation a frequent stage for outrageous behavior. One prisoner, using smuggled matches and toilet paper, managed to set his mattress on fire. When staff rushed to open his cell door, they found he had jammed the lock. By the time they were able to open the door, the inmate was barely breathing and covered in ashes and soot. The officers dragged him out of the smoke-filled room. The inmate regained consciousness on the cold cement floor outside his cell, looked up at the officers who had just saved his life, and said, "That will teach you people to quit fucking with my canteen order."

Another unstable Segregation inmate was Alan Eddington, a downright bestial man who possessed a strong will to hurt people. He was well-conditioned and powerful from untold hours pumping iron until his skin bulged with muscles. Eddington was also dangerous and unpredictable. I tried to speak to him several times, but he rarely communicated with staff. Eddington seemed ready to attack guards at any moment, and we had to watch his every step. In one incident, he appeared peaceful, then unexpectedly spun around and drove his fist into an officer's windpipe. This earned him an attempted murder conviction to add to his resumé of sentences.

Another inmate prosecuted in outside courts for assaulting staff was William Jacks. Short and stocky yet supremely athletic, Jacks was like a bomb just waiting to explode. He was doing time for several barbaric assaults, and prison had not been able to scrub this violence out of him. He lived in Segregation for several years where guards used considerable precaution every time they came into contact with him—yet he still managed to assault twelve correctional officers in eighteen months. One day, as several staff members escorted him from the recreation yard to his cell, Jacks suddenly turned and headbutted an officer in the face. Even the restraints and number of officers didn't stop him. He still found a way to hurt someone.

Eddington and Jacks were among the worst predators. Some years ago, we transferred them to the Federal Penitentiary in Marion, Illinois. The warden was a friend of mine and agreed on the transfers. It wasn't that we couldn't control Eddington and Jacks; it was more that we needed a break from them. Those two didn't look so bad once they were gone, however; we knew there would be others to take their place, cons like Herbert Cummings and Manfred Locks.

Cummings I already knew from my years at a county facility where he had been a regular. He had a sour attitude along with numerous physical and mental problems. He never got along with anyone—inmates or staff—and spent his time destroying his living space. He often broke glass and desecrated walls and windows. As difficult as it was to deal with him, I always pitied Cummings. He had no friends and always believed someone had wronged him. He was probably the most disagreeable person I have ever met, but I cannot recall him ever physically injuring anyone.

During Cummings's last stay at Oak Park Heights, he served his entire sentence in the Segregation Unit. On the day of his release, he carved up the windows, tore apart his bedding, and flooded his cell. When he was brought upstairs to the holding cell, he began to destroy this cell as well. I found Cummings banging his fists against the walls, spit trickling down the windows. I told Cummings that if he did one more damaging thing, we would call the local sheriff and have him arrested for destruction of state property. Instead of leaving a free man, he would be arrested and taken to the local jail. He calmed down and left quietly, but I don't think the outside world was ready for him.

Cummings died a short time later. He was a street person, and I can only imagine the suffering he must have gone through. We never heard how he died, but it probably wasn't under the best circumstances. His obituary bore the touching statement, "This poor lost soul has finally found his way home."

Unlike Cummings, Manfred Locks was a dangerous man with a violent agenda. He was serving time for a burglary in Wisconsin and had been transferred to Oak Park Heights in an attempt to control his savage behavior. In one incident, Locks managed to deceive guards into thinking he was safely locked in his cell after taking a shower, but he was actually hiding in a shower stall, waiting to attack the first staff person who appeared. When an officer entered, Locks assaulted him with a towel rack. Locks inflicted serious lacerations all over the head of the officer, who managed to escape more of Locks's wrath. Locks didn't know who he was going to attack and likely didn't care. He simply wanted to hurt someone—even though he was serving the last six months of his incarceration. Fulfilling his addiction to violence was more important than his impending freedom.

Alan Eddington, William Jacks, Herbert Cummings, and Manfred Locks were all troublesome inmates, but none of them came close to Richard Samuels. What made Samuels different was his remarkable ability to sustain violent and aggressive activity over a prolonged period of time. He was a one-man wrecking crew with an incredible ability to demolish jails and prisons.

Samuels's reputation preceded him. Transfers are usually routine affairs that generate little concern beyond the normal precautions accompanying all new admissions. We knew, however, that Samuels was being transferred to Oak Park Heights because few facilities in the country could control him. We were told he had literally dismantled a small jail piece by piece. He was described as a human destruction machine with a motor stuck in high gear.

Samuels's reputation was right on target. When he arrived,

his entire person seemed to exude hostility and hatred to other human beings—especially if they wore a uniform. Right away, he informed us we were in for a hard time. "You've never faced the likes of me," he told us. And he was right. The brand-new prison was like Disneyland to Samuels. He awoke every day looking forward to taking on new destructive challenges, whether people or property. He had all these shiny, unused things to break, tear, rip, smash, wreck, and destroy. That was Richard Samuels, a monster in human form.

I came into contact with Samuels when I was the prison's Internal Affairs Investigator during those early years. My responsibilities included investigating disturbances, major staff or inmate misconduct, or out-of-the-ordinary occurrences—and when Samuel lived here, every day was out of the ordinary. His drive and determination amazed me. He possessed an incredible desire to accomplish what he set out to do. In a different lifetime, that determination could have been harnessed to a positive end. As it was, it seemed like such a waste to focus all this persistence toward such negative results.

One of Samuels's many skills was obtaining unauthorized items and converting them into weapons or tools. Once, staff executed a thorough search of him, his cell, and the area around his cell, but within a few hours, while isolated in his cell, he had accumulated more weapons, tools, and other objects than I could have gathered from a hardware store. It was incredible. He had wire, screws, bolts, metal, and paper—from where, we didn't know. Either he retrieved them from hiding places so cunning we probably never will discover them, or he convinced other inmates to pass items to him.

Samuels's innate ability to recruit inmates in support of

his mission was another feature that made him stand out. He was like the captain of a team with everyone waiting to respond to his leadership and direction. This tremendous power made him even more dangerous.

The solitary confinement section comprises just seven cells on the lower tier and represents the highest level of security within Oak Park Heights. It is at the far end of the Segregation Unit, across the main floor from the sally port. To reach this section, you pass the other living areas and descend several steps to a steel door. As you enter the cell area, the door closes behind you, trapping you inside a small area adjacent to the seven cells. It's a tight space with only enough room for a steel table, which is bolted to the floor so it can't serve as a weapon. This area is where the section inmates take their daily hour of exercise. Samuels spent all of his stay in the Segregation Unit under solitary confinement. He was allowed nothing in his cell but his clothing. Anything else he would destroy or use as a weapon.

Samuels didn't work alone. His disruptive behavior won attention and respect from other inmates, and this soon thrust him into a leadership role. Before long, he had five hostile, aggressive cons in solitary following his lead. Samuels excelled at picking a most offensive team. They were all devious, committed followers with several murders on their resumés, and they looked up to Samuels like a charismatic leader of a cult of violence.

Samuels and his followers were originally housed in neighboring solitary confinement cells. The cells were largely soundproof, so Samuels passed on his "teachings" by screaming loud enough for the others to hear him. He instructed them on what to do, and soon we had chaos. They broke up sinks and toilets, tore electrical plates from walls, smashed mirrors and windows, ruined hinges, doors, light fixtures, wall vents, and anything else in their way. The damage was extensive, the repairs costly and time-consuming. Every day they were charged with prison rule violations that only extended their stays in the Segregation Unit.

The summer that Samuels came to Oak Park Heights was the only time in my career that my job responsibilities created a knot in my stomach every day. As I walked into the unit each morning, I knew there was an unpleasant experience ahead. I can only imagine how the officers who had to work near Samuels eight hours a day felt. He kept staff on guard every minute. On one occasion, he was able to free himself from handcuffs and waist chains and punch a correctional officer in the face. The other inmates idolized him, and he worked hard to keep his image intact. The five inmates led by him were relentless in their efforts to keep from being controlled. One morning, I entered the unit to find three of Samuels's accomplices sitting on their cell floor chained around the sink post. The staff simply had no other way to control them. The inmates had been breaking up their cells and, after being moved to different cells, started to destroy their new locations. Chaining them to the sink was the only way to restrain them.

Oak Park Heights was under no obligation to keep this human destructor. The Vermont prison system had transferred Samuels to Minnesota as part of the Interstate Compact, an arrangement administered by most state corrections departments. The Interstate Compact is based on mutual agreement, and we could have shipped Samuels back to Vermont any time we wished. But Warden Frank Wood had a different idea. He reasoned that if Samuels was one of the most violent and destructive inmates in the country, why not use some of his negative expertise to our advantage? We would keep him as an unpaid consultant to assist us in learning how to reconstruct our cells.

Samuels continued his resistive and damaging behavior, and we repaired his destruction but always in a manner that created a sturdier cell. Sinks were remade and reinforced; they could no longer be pulled out of the wall, broken up, or destroyed. Electrical plates were removed from the walls, and toilets were rebuilt and reconfigured so they could no longer be smashed. We installed shut-off valves that stopped the water supply after a toilet is flushed a second time. We replaced lights and windows with unbreakable materials. We cut a slot in the steel door to restrain the inmate at the door when staff needed to enter the cell. Door hinges were enlarged and carefully secured. Special steel flaps were installed over the cell door windows, and steel grates were installed to provide additional barriers between inmates and staff.

Throughout this process, we meticulously documented Samuel's wreckage. One morning, shortly after he broke the window out of his cell door, I arrived with a camera. I snapped photographs of the damage as Samuels hollered and growled profanities. In the few months I knew him, he never spoke a civil word to me. One of the pictures I took shows Samuels giving me the finger. It was the only clear communication he ever managed.

Later, when inmates filed a civil lawsuit claiming the prison was using unlawful practices to restrain them, the records and photographs of Samuels's destruction became key evidence in our defense. Based partly on these materials, the federal court found their claims lacking in merit, and the case was dismissed. This was just part of the positive legacy left by Samuels's horrifying behavior.

Eventually, Samuels completed his consulting work. We placed him in cell number 101, where he was fully controlled and contained. There was nothing he could destroy, and for the first time since his arrival, he was totally frustrated. We built twelve more cells like 101. We called them our modified cells.

With nothing else to do, Samuels resorted to smearing his own excrement on the walls and throwing it around his cell. In his way of thinking, it was the only way to get back some of his perceived power.

Shortly after Samuels was controlled in cell 101, I escorted his attorney to the Segregation Unit for a visit with his client. They spoke through the rectangular food-pass cut in the cement wall, slightly below eye level. Suddenly, the attorney dropped his eyes and backed away from the cell. Samuels had placed a pile of human feces on the shelf. I don't know what his message was, but it wasn't a pleasant one.

On another occasion, the unit supervisor and I were in the area near Samuels's cell, and he was still trying to convince us that he was in charge. It was tough to convince him he wasn't. Here he was locked in the newly built cell, totally confined, without anything to smash or break so throwing excrement was all he had left. Yet still he shouted, "Why don't you go upstairs and tell Wood who is running this prison?" His only relief would come from good behavior, and he was not about to lower himself to that standard.

Once we had learned all we could about building indestructible cells from Samuels, Frank Wood arranged for his return transfer. Vermont officials, unable to place Samuels in any other state in the nation, came to pick him up. They shackled Samuels in full restraints, then loaded him into the backseat of a four-wheel-drive Chevrolet Suburban. Oak Park Heights's captain of security and I watched as they headed down the driveway. I stood there thinking, Samuels will have that Suburban dismantled by the time they hit the Wisconsin border, just a few miles away.

Many years later, I heard of an unprecedented interstate transfer—five inmates in exchange for a single prisoner. It was like a sporting world trade, five utility players for one star. But in this trade, Tennessee was trading five of its most aggressive murderers for one convict from Vermont. I also heard that Allan Greeley, the Tennessee transfer coordinator, was seen as a hero in his department for executing this wonderful deal.

When our state transfer coordinator asked the name of this one person, Greeley checked and called back. The inmate's name was Richard Samuels.

Within sixty days, Greeley called Vermont and asked for his five murderers back. "Come as quickly as possible," he told them, "and get this rotten son of a bitch out of here."

Fatal
Attractions

The letter was a plea, heartfelt and loving. Over several handwritten pages, the author, an Ohio woman, asked us to please release prisoner Gerald Anders. She detailed her caring relationship with him and the supportive home she was prepared to set up for the two of them. She described how she had come to know and deeply understand this man, mentioning their unusual connection and growing dependence upon each other. She wrote of the special love that had developed between them, and her confidence that this bond would guide them to a fulfilling life together. A transfer of supervision to Ohio, she argued, would be in his best interests, and she could provide a strong support system for him there.

I was impressed by the sincere tone of the letter. Her words were saturated with an emotional intensity unusual to letters concerning offenders. There was little doubt she was honest about her desire for a life with Anders and felt genuine devotion to him.

Her final remarks, however, were what set this correspondence apart from any other. As she brought her plea to an end, she wrote, "and the reason our love is so special is that we have never met."

I set the letter down and thought of her compassion—and her naïveté. She was obviously a woman with hopes and dreams, but also with a frightening lack of insight into what her future would be like with a person such as Anders.

Gerald Anders was a violent sex offender with a serious criminal history, including convictions for assault, burglary, kidnapping, and rape with the use of a weapon. With this kind of past, he had a precarious future. He had recently been granted parole, but almost immediately violated the parole requirements. When Oregon police apprehended him, they took him from a vehicle with its interior splattered in blood. Police found human hair and signs of a struggle, but they never found a victim. Without solid evidence of a criminal act, Anders faced no more than the technical violation of his parole. Only Anders would ever know what grisly events took place in that car.

He was returned to Minnesota to face parole revocation proceedings, and it was then that I received the earnest plea from his girlfriend in Ohio. She apparently had learned nothing of the brutal heartlessness of his past during their correspondence and phone calls. She thought she wanted to spend the rest of her life with him.

At the hearing, Anders's parole was revoked. Between his history of violent sexual behavior and the circumstances under which he was arrested, he represented a significant risk to the public. He was ordered to serve the rest of his sentence, which was several more years of incarceration. Society had a right to be safe from the likes of Gerald Anders.

The years passed and the end of his sentence neared. Anders was allowed a furlough to secure work and a place to live. He was about to be a free man in a matter of days.

But the furlough was a failure. He absconded and, armed with a weapon, committed a series of monstrous sexual assaults on three victims. Gerald Anders is now incarcerated for the balance of his life. I can only imagine what might have occurred if Anders had been released to live with his girlfriend in Ohio. Likely, she would have been his next victim.

Why would a person be willing to devote her life to a convicted sex offender whom she has never met? Why would she open her home and risk everything?

It was just another of many fatal attractions between Big House inmates and women on the outside.

These fatal attractions are all too common. For certain women on the outside, convicted felons hold an irresistible magnetism. These women seem driven by a need to help the downtrodden, nurture the scorned, the oppressed, and the wicked. They act out of compassion and love, faith and belief—even as the object of their affection manipulates and lies.

I witnessed one of these liaisons some years ago when I was the Executive Officer of Adult Release for the Minnesota Department of Corrections. One of my responsibilities was to conduct parole revocation hearings. One day I received a long-distance telephone call from a concerned woman in North Dakota who said her husband, Minnesota parolee Jerry Fowler, had landed in the local county jail. When the local authorities checked his record, they found an active fugitive warrant for Fowler; he had absconded supervision several months ago. His wife hoped the Department of Corrections would not extradite Fowler back to Minnesota to face parole violations. She spoke of the life they were setting up in North Dakota and expressed her confidence they could get past his current problem with the local police.

The odd part about our exchange was her lack of knowledge about her husband. I asked her some basic questions about his background, only to find that she didn't know what crime he had committed, how much time he had served on his latest offense, or when he had been released from prison. The only thing she seemed to know about Fowler was that he was a convicted sex offender. But she also didn't know about his long list of victims.

Because she was so unsure about his offense history, I asked her how long they had been married. "One week," she answered. They had married in the county jail after his recent arrest. Surprised, I asked how long she had known Jerry Fowler. She told me to hold and spoke to someone in the background: "Mavis, there is a guy on the phone who wants to know how long I've known Jerry. When was that carnival in town?"

These relationships are heart-rending. She was just beginning to experience the anguish of life with a person like Fowler, and one can only imagine what the future would hold.

As I encountered these troublesome relationships through the years, I soon learned that as bad as one sounded, another would come along and be even more disturbing. Then I learned firsthand about a relationship that eclipsed all others. In my opinion, no fatal attraction will ever be more alarming or disheartening.

I met the woman when I was a member of the Minnesota State Parole Board. She set up an appointment with me to discuss her boyfriend's approaching release. In our meeting, I found her to be a pleasant professional woman in her early thirties, attractively dressed in her business attire. She was soft-spoken and polite, yet obviously distressed about something. She confessed that her inmate boyfriend, Bruce Clemmons, had made a troubling request. Her own background was free from criminal activity, and I suspect this relationship was her first experience with a convicted felon.

Clemmons was a convicted sex offender with a sad history of deviant sexual behavior. What made his case particularly bizarre was his sexual fixation with dogs. His file contained information about his sexual contact with numerous dogs in the area where he lived. The reports indicated that the contact may have included more than a thousand dogs over a ten-year period.

The problem now facing his girlfriend was Clemmons's plan upon release. He told her to purchase a dog and get sexually active with the animal so they could be "ready" for him when he was released.

This woman, a vulnerable and caring person, had become so romantically involved with a deranged sex offender that she was actually in a quandary about whether to start a sexual relationship with a dog! This was Clemmons's plan for starting their life together in the community. She seemed so defenseless against his request that the suggestion alone should have been a crime.

I tried my best to counsel her out of the relationship, but my efforts were fruitless. Some months later, I read a discipline report from the Stillwater Correctional Facility indicating that Clemmons and his girlfriend were barred from future visits at the prison due to their behavior during a community awards banquet with special invited guests. The report explained that they had been caught having sexual relations during the program. Obviously something was radically wrong with the setting, the security, and the relationship between Clemmons and his visitor. This woman's infatuation with a freakish sex offender had become so overpowering that she was willing to sacrifice her own dignity to fulfill his wants as he neared his release date several months ahead.

A couple years later, I ran into her at a gas station. We didn't speak. I imagine she was too embarrassed by all that had occurred. The tragic affair had finally come to an end when Clemmons died of a heart attack a few years after release. This painful relationship was over, but the suffering would likely never be forgotten.

The visiting room is one of the most disturbing areas of the prison. Here, inmates have the opportunity to see friends, relatives, and loved ones. And it's here that some of these twisted fatal attractions develop.

To be placed on an offender's visiting list, an intensive background check is performed and qualifications must be met. The visiting room is a critical area for security to prevent drugs from being smuggled inside. Anything from marijuana to crack cocaine can find a path into prison when a devious inmate and a dishonest or coerced visitor work together.

A few years ago, we arrested a nineteen-year-old woman as she entered the facility to visit her prisoner boyfriend. Our intelligence information warned us that she would be bringing drugs to the boyfriend. She was apprehended in possession of the contraband and placed under arrest. She was devastated. Previously, she had no criminal record, a past without any major problems. All that changed. She was now taken into custody and booked into the local county jail for attempting to introduce drugs into a supermax prison.

This was an all-too-common situation. Some years ago, a study examined visitors who had been arrested for attempting to bring drugs to inmates. Most of the arrests were of women with no previous criminal background. They had formed trusting relationships with the offenders and had been threatened or manipulated into committing a felony.

This young woman arrested for drug possession later told us she had met the inmate through a friend and fallen in love. They planned to marry upon his release in December. Yet he had lied to her and ruined her crime-free life. The prisoner was serving a sentence for first degree murder, and although it was true he would be eligible for parole in December, it was thirty years from this particular December.

Countless devious and disgusting tales emerge from the visiting area. Here, drugs enter the prison environment by some of the most despicable methods, with hiding places ranging from personal undergarments to baby diapers.

Typically, the visitor conceals the drugs in a balloon. During a hug or kiss, the visitor transfers the stash to the inmate, who swallows the balloon whole. The normal digestive process allows the balloon to be excreted, and the prisoner then retrieves it from his toilet. Another method is to simply force regurgitation as soon as he returns to the cell. It sounds crude, but it's the reality of prison.

If undetected by staff, this is a cunning way to smuggle and conceal contraband. However, one problem is that the balloon can easily break inside the inmate's stomach. A bellyful of heroin or cocaine wreaks serious havoc. This precise scenario occurred on two occasions several years ago at the Minnesota Correctional Facility-Stillwater. One inmate suffered serious medical problems as the drugs permeated his digestive system. The other inmate died from the overdose.

After the two broken-balloon incidents, the department revised security procedures for visiting day. Visitors and prisoners used to be allowed nearly limitless physical contact. They could sit next to each other, hug, and kiss, all of which provided an avenue for drugs to pass into the prison. Visiting rooms were equipped with vending machines, and the candy and soft drinks provided more ways to swallow drugs undetected.

To restrict the ability to pass drugs, the vending machines were removed and the policy for contact significantly altered. A visitor is now allowed a quick kiss on the cheek and two brief hugs with the inmate—one upon entrance and one at the visit's conclusion. No other physical contact is allowed during the visit, and the seating arrangement requires space between inmate and visitor. Visits are closely monitored by staff and often by security cameras to make sure these restrictions are followed. These changes have been instrumental in reducing the amount of contraband entering the prison system.

❖❖❖

Though the improved procedures create a safer environment, the visiting room continues to be one of the saddest places imaginable. It is particularly difficult to watch children visiting incarcerated parents or relatives. The children seem so innocent and unaware of their surroundings.

I recall watching some happy youngsters bouncing on the lap of their father, who was in prison for killing their mother. He was a quiet and generally unnoticeable individual, but he had murdered the woman, cut her up, and used a garbage disposal to get rid of the body. I wondered if the children knew what he had done.

Knowing the details of their crimes, I often found it a wonder some of these offenders ever received visitors. Maybe their crime was a brutal rape, a vicious murder, or the molestation of a child. How could someone fall in love or stay in love with someone who has committed such heinous acts? The crime often doesn't appear to matter. All seems forgotten. "Live for the moment" is the philosophy, with little regard for the past or future. It doesn't make sense but this mindset exists every day in prisons.

Though I found the majority of these relationships perplexing and sad, some seemed to transcend the sordidness of the situations. I always admired one devoted wife who stayed married to her dying inmate husband and telephoned him from another state for many years. She was as caring as she could be from a lengthy distance away. Their relationship was real, loving, and long lasting. Yet he was a murderer who had been locked up most of his life.

It didn't matter to her. She loved him.

Unholy Alliance

Never, under any circumstances, share any aspect of your personal life with an inmate." This is a prison officer's cardinal rule. The directive is driven into the mind of every correctional officer who works in a prison system. It is an essential part of each officer's training. The caution is so clear and direct that no one could ever doubt the message.

Inmates cannot be trusted. When an inmate does get hold of personal information, he will—in almost every circumstance—use it against the officer. No Minnesota case proves this true more than the unholy alliance formed between Correctional Officer Bill Anthony and federal inmate Marshall Walker.

As the first Internal Affairs Investigator at the newly opened Oak Park Heights prison, I performed the background check on Bill Anthony in spring 1982. Anthony had worked as a correctional officer in the Oklahoma prison system, and his references praised him as an outstanding employee who was competent and well liked by his colleagues.

We hired him in July and quickly found him to be all that was promised—bright, articulate, and enthusiastic. Anthony fit in well with the staff. He had a positive way about him, a friendly personality that attracted colleagues. His charisma and experience made him easy to like and look to for leadership. And he carried out assignments with polish and professionalism. We felt fortunate to have him.

Anthony was assigned to work in the Segregation Unit, one of the toughest tours of duty available. During the prison's first few years, we had some difficult times in this intense setting.

✦✦✦

The destruction and eventual remodeling of the cells during Richard Samuels's visit was stressful and cumbersome. Our staff was relatively young and inexperienced, and they were constantly challenged trying to control Samuels and the other antagonistic offenders.

Working in Segregation demands staff members to be their very best every minute of every shift. The offenders in this unit are the worst of the worst. They are high risk, incorrigible, and know how to cause problems. Rules and regulations must be followed explicitly to prevent injury. Control is the highest priority and deviation from policy risks serious harm.

Even under the most precautionary conditions, inmates still sometimes manage to assault staff. Inmates can be predatory, waiting patiently for the precise time and place to attack. This is why Segregation requires the highest quality staff, the best trained and the most trusted. Officers in this unit rely on each other more so than any other prison assignment.

In one potentially serious incident at Oak Parks Heights, a handcuffed inmate managed to pull away from an officer's grip and, turning the metal handcuffs into a weapon, strike the officer repeatedly on the back of the head. Though the inmate was quickly subdued in this instance, these attacks can turn deadly.

That is exactly what happened in 1983 in the Control Unit of the United States Penitentiary at Marion, Illinois. In separate incidents within eight hours of each other in the prison's most secure unit, inmates attacked and killed two guards. They were dangerous offenders who waited for their opportunity, then struck, carefully executing their murderous plans.

+ + +

Officer Bill Anthony seemed up to the task of the Segregation Unit. His experience in Oklahoma was invaluable, and it didn't take long for him to make significant contributions to our procedures. He performed well under demanding circumstances.

Then he met double murderer Marshall Walker.

Walker was one of those felons with the outward appearance of a "nice guy." He was a model inmate, friendly and talkative, one not likely to cause trouble. His good behavior had earned him prime work assignments out of his cell and in close contact with the staff. During his work time, he spoke with Anthony of his life on the outside, describing it as filled with wealth and glamour.

In contrast, Anthony's life had recently taken a turn for the worse. He had become financially strapped. His marriage was failing. He was separated from his children. He was drinking too much and abusing drugs. As his personal life fell apart, Anthony did not turn to friends or family, a counselor or religious leader. Instead, he turned to a convicted murderer.

Months later, Anthony would describe Walker as a "high roller who was easy to talk to, and someone who lived in the fast lane." In fact, Walker was smart, cunning, and dangerous. Federal authorities were temporarily detaining Walker at Oak Park Heights pending transfer to another prison. He was an accomplished and manipulative felon with a plan, and Anthony was to become a major player.

Anthony's work assignment required him to spend long days in the unit, and he spent a lot of time around Walker, who was a floor cleaner and thus often out of his cell during the day. Their routine conversations took a wrong turn. Instead of communicating with Walker on a purely professional level, Anthony broke the cardinal rule. Disregarding the most protected of all correctional officer practices, Anthony brought Walker into the sacredness of his personal life. Anthony allowed his judgment to become contaminated by alcohol and drug abuse, as well as a misguided belief that his association with Walker would somehow enhance his perception of himself. He was wrong. Instead, he became a hopeless pawn in a scheme of manipulation and conspiracy.

As Christmas approached, Anthony continued to outwardly perform his duties at the prison without difficulty. Inwardly, however, he worried about the looming holiday season and how few dollars he had for his children's Christmas presents.

The more contact he had with Walker, the more he became enamored with the seemingly glamorous felon. During their conversations, Anthony was able to escape, however temporarily, some of his personal troubles. Walker bragged about his wealth and his status in the world of criminals. Anthony listened, captivated.

If Anthony had followed what he learned in the academy, it may have saved his career. Instead, he lost all control, talking freely with Walker about his financial difficulties and even some of his after work activities. He gave Walker a picture of his life outside the prison—a tragic error on his part. Walker absorbed it all.

Walker tracked the dates, places, and activities that Anthony confided to him. Slowly, he began to feed the information back to Anthony. The officer had given Walker so much personal information he couldn't remember exactly what he had told him. Anthony quickly became frightened. The inmate named details such as when and where Anthony went bowling.

Anthony wondered if Walker was having him followed in the community. He couldn't believe Walker knew that much about his personal life.

Then Anthony began to get calls during his off-duty hours from Walker's friends on the outside. His personal life was falling apart and becoming intertwined with his work life. He was scared.

Walker had Anthony right where he wanted him. It was time to step up the pressure. He demanded a favor—one that would turn Anthony from officer to criminal. He asked Anthony to smuggle in contraband—hacksaw blades and a handcuff key—in exchange for one thousand dollars.

At first, Anthony refused. He wanted out of the relationship. He wanted help from his fellow officers. But he felt too closely connected to Walker by now to entrust anyone with his troubles. He had violated sacred policy. He was afraid and desperate.

The worst possible scenario was now in place in the most dangerous unit of Minnesota's supermax prison. A trusted correctional officer had befriended an inmate and become entangled in a criminal conspiracy. His family life was slipping away. He was chemically addicted and out of money. He was in pain outside of work and in trouble at work. His life was out of control.

He began to cave. He considered Walker's request. It might be a way out. He was still fascinated by Walker's wealth and status in the criminal world, and this might be a chance to get closer to Walker. And he could resolve some of his financial difficulties.

Finally, he agreed.

◆ ◆ ◆

Jethro's Char House is a sports bar tucked in the corner of a small shopping center in the Twin Cities suburb of White Bear Lake. It is located some fifteen miles northeast of St. Paul and ten miles west of the Oak Park Heights prison. What happened in this parking lot late one evening changed Anthony's life forever.

To go through with this criminal activity, Anthony sedated himself with a full day of drinking and arrived at the parking lot in a state of drunken despair. Here, one of Walker's friends handed Anthony a paper bag containing a cigar case and a roll of money totaling one thousand dollars. The case was small, just a few inches long, and contained a handcuff key and several short hacksaw blades.

The next day, Anthony stuffed the cigar case into his boot and practiced walking in front of his bathroom mirror. He did not want to draw attention to himself by walking with a different stride. Yet deep down, he also felt sure he would be caught. The administration periodically searched staff members as they entered prison to begin their work shift. If he were caught, his career would be over, but the dangerous contraband would never be in Walker's possession.

There was no search that day. Anthony successfully smuggled the hacksaw blades and handcuff key into Segregation. He approached Walker, who was working out of his cell, and set the cigar case on a table.

"Never ask me to do anything for you again," Anthony said, and walked away.

He figured their dealings were finished.

✦ ✦ ✦

Anthony's problems up to this point were minimal compared to what was ahead. Just days after receiving these dangerous items, Walker would be transferred to the Wright County Jail in western Minnesota to face new criminal charges. In the meantime, Walker hid the cigar case in his rectum, where it went undetected during routine cell and body searches.

Then, he waited.

There was no way out of Oak Park Heights. The key and blades were of little value to Walker in his current setting. Tests have shown it would take approximately twelve thousand hacksaw blades to cut through the steel bars of the prison windows. In the near-impossible event that an inmate did make it out of his cell, he would face a steep wall with a detection system on the roof. If he made it to the top of the wall and over the roof, he faced a buffer zone of 160 acres, surrounded by a sensor-controlled double cyclone fence, lined with massive coils of razor ribbon.

Walker had to find a way out from a different location. He would do exactly that.

When Walker was transferred to the county jail, body searches failed to detect the escape materials concealed in his rectum. The moment he was placed in the custody of the county jail authorities, he began planning his escape. The security here was significantly less than at Oak Park Heights, and soon Walker found a way out by cutting through the ceiling of his cell. Using the hacksaw blades provided by Anthony, Walker escaped.

✦✦✦

Three days later, a statewide manhunt captured Marshall Walker near one of the beautiful lakes in Minneapolis. Upon interrogation, Walker shamelessly revealed Anthony's role in the escape. At first, it seemed no more than an absurd statement by a double murderer against a credible officer.

Warden Frank Wood and our internal affairs investigator called in the Minnesota Bureau of Criminal Apprehension to help perform the unpleasant task of investigating a correctional officer for conspiring with a convicted murderer. As the assistant to the warden, I was also part of the investigation. It soon became apparent because of detailed information provided by Walker that Anthony was involved. But proving it would be difficult.

Weeks of investigation brought forth no strong evidence tying Anthony to Walker's escape. We became more frustrated as the days went by.

By far the most frustrated was the investigator assigned to the case from the Bureau. As the case's formal closing date loomed, Wood, our internal affairs investigator, and I pursued the case relentlessly, pressuring the state investigator to continue. We were now positive Anthony was involved.

For Anthony, these weeks as a suspect were the worst part of the whole ordeal. He would run into me and Wood walking around the prison and try to hold a normal conversation with us.

"I knew you knew and you didn't say anything," he told me later, "and that was the worst."

Anthony finally confessed. Weeks of constant pressure broke him down. He told us everything. He was honest and contrite. Mostly, however, he was ashamed.

I will never forget the day the news of Anthony's arrest circulated around the prison. Local law enforcement booked him into the county jail. Our staff was overwhelmed at the news, and at first, there was intense support for the well-liked officer. Staff members were appalled and outraged. They blamed the administration for seizing one of their own.

Before long, details of the arrest leaked out. The prison went into a total state of shock. A fellow officer had compromised the safety of others for his own profit. A respected friend and colleague had done the unthinkable. He had conspired with an inmate and, in the process, put their lives on the line. The news was devastating.

After the initial shock, the staff became demoralized when they learned more of Anthony's immoral and illegal acts. Though Walker never used the handcuff key, it represented the highest level of security breach. To provide it to an inmate was unforgivable. What if Walker had used the key to get out of restraints at Oak Park Heights? What if he had then used the hacksaw blade to slit an officer's throat?

The staff's rage against the administration was then turned against Anthony. His betrayal sold out his fellow workers, all for one thousand dollars. He dismissed their safety in an act of selfishness. It wasn't right and they wanted answers. Unfortunately, there weren't any to give. There would never be a justification for Anthony's betrayal.

In the end, Anthony was found guilty and sentenced to prison. Frank Wood, the Commissioner, the Deputy Commissioner of Corrections, our prison investigator, and I were present for the sentencing. We wanted to be sure the judge would not mistake our expectations for this sentence.

Former Correctional Officer Bill Anthony had now changed sides. Instead of protecting the public, he was now watched, guarded, and secured. Correctional officers were instructed to beware of him like all the others. He was an inmate, like the murderers, rapists, robbers, and thieves. He had become one of them.

Bill Anthony's picture still hangs on the wall with the other training academy graduates from Academy Class Number Five at the Oak Park Heights prison. He is pointed out to new staff as an example of how a career can be ruined.

However, Anthony found a way to make some amends. During his incarceration at the Stillwater correctional facility, Anthony agreed to make a training video detailing what he had done. In the video, Anthony speaks candidly of his relationship with Walker. He discusses the hours of conversations, the months of personal interaction. He describes the fear that developed as Walker brought him closer to the elements of his criminal world. He reflects upon the role drinking and drugs played. He describes the final crime and the ruin it brought to his family, his career, and his personal integrity.

In making this valuable training tool, a remorseful Anthony assists new officers, helping them avoid getting caught up in a similar scheme. Anthony, in some small fashion, found a way to atone for what he had done. Perhaps he reclaimed some of his self respect. Certainly, I respect him for his fortitude and honesty.

Anthony served a little over a year in prison and was released. After his release, I never heard from him again.

The Clever, the Humorous, the Cons, and the Stupid

On a typical weekday, inmates in the Industry Area work on a variety of projects, such as silk screening, notebook binding, and sewing. They're always under the watchful eye of a correctional officer, who observes them from a security bubble. This station is enclosed by reinforced glass and contains a small cutout at waist level for communication. One day, I stood outside the security bubble watching the daily routine of the area. A guard sat at his post inside the bubble observing the area. An inmate approached the glass, leaned down to the opening, and said, "I'll have a cheeseburger, fries, and a Coke."

The stern-faced officer sent the inmate back to his work area, but I smiled. It amazes me that inmates, absent of all freedoms, can still have a sense of humor. I appreciated his wit, if only for a second. After all, the security bubble did look like a fast food drive-through.

The stories that emerge from a career in corrections are often frightening and depressing. But some are interesting, others amazing, and a few downright funny. Over the years, I have categorized the most unusual and amusing crimes, criminals, and incidents into a list: the humorous, the clever, the cons, and the stupid. You won't find these examples in sociological studies or criminology textbooks; they are my own examples, based on thirty-five years of personal observations.

The Humorous

Another amusing moment at Oak Park Heights came during the annual visit from a committee of Minnesota legislators. Because the state legislature oversees the Department of Corrections, we always took the committee on a thorough tour deep into the bowels of the institution.

One afternoon, we entered a room adjacent to the cellblock where we stored various types of restraint equipment hung on the walls. I explained to the politicians that we routinely use this equipment in the Segregation Unit to control violent offenders. I pointed out a large, flat board equipped with heavy-duty Velcro straps and described some of the behavior that might earn an inmate time strapped to the board. An inmate might have been banging his head against the wall, I explained, or cutting himself with a sharp object, or attempting to inflict some other bodily harm. Or he might have broken a window, flooded his cell or damaged it in some other way. The board, I said, helps physically restrain such inmates for a period of time, in order to get them back under control.

A legislator interrupted me. As always, the state had sent several new members to see the prison. "I understand the need for controlling violent inmates," the disturbed legislator said, "but I just don't think it's right to bring someone into this room, strap them to the board, and let them hang on the wall."

I was astonished, but managed to calmly explain that we take the board off the wall, bring it to the offender's cell, and place it on the floor to restrain him. I guess it is important that we give the tours.

I'm not always the one laughing. Sometimes, the joke is on me, such as the time many years ago when my friend Don Peterson and I were working part-time for the Minnesota State Fair Police Department.

On a warm summer evening, a young man at the fair was taken into custody after a loud and disorderly fracas. It turned out he had walked away from his residence, a minimum-security mental health institution located in northern Ramsey

County. His mental condition didn't seem to warrant putting him through the court process, and rather than taking him downtown for booking, the night captain directed Don and me to return him to his institution.

The police captain told us that the man, Ivan, was sitting in the back of an unmarked police vehicle. As we approached the car, I saw the largest, scariest-looking human being I have ever seen. He was huge, with a close-shaven head and a mean, disgruntled look on his face. His eyes were a cold, cloudy blue that stared straight back into your eyes without blinking. He sent a chill up my back, and all I could think of was "Ivan the Terrible."

I slid into the driver's seat and turned the rearview mirror on Ivan. Don sat in the front passenger seat and turned to watch him. As I backed out of the police department lot, I heard a bloodcurdling scream and saw a woman running toward us. She reached the car and leaned in. "I am his mother," she said quietly, "and I want you to know that he is very dangerous. Please be careful."

It was a long drive to the institution. I had the mirror glued to Ivan, and Don had one hand on his gun.

Ivan never said a word, and we finally arrived at the institution, where we were met by the director, Dr. Dave Gladdings. He greeted Ivan, then took us into his office and told us about Ivan's history, the other residents, and the facility's purpose. He said he had been the director for several years and had a background of working with mentally ill patients. His experience, communication skills, and advanced degrees appeared to make him well-suited for his important position. He was gracious and professional, and even gave us a complete tour of the residence and grounds.

After about an hour, we thanked Dr. Gladdings for his hospitality and left. On the drive back, we decided we should have gotten some type of paperwork proving Ivan was returned. In case he wandered off again, we wanted the record to be clear that we had turned him over to their custody.

Back at the facility, the director's office was locked. We found a maintenance worker buffing a corridor floor and asked him if Dr. Gladdings might be available. Oddly, he had never heard of Dr. Gladdings. Confused, we explained who we were, how we had returned Ivan, and had met with the director.

"Was the man you met about forty years old and wearing a dark blue suit with a red tie?" the worker asked.

Yes, we responded.

He informed us that the man in the blue suit was not Dr. Gladdings. There was no Dr. Gladdings. The person with whom we had toured the facility was a mental patient named Horace Schmitt. He had lived at the residence for many years and believed he was in charge. Unbelievable! We checked on Ivan to make sure he was safely where he was supposed to be, obtained our discharge report, and quickly left the premises.

Don and I are not the only officers to ever get hoodwinked. One of my favorite recollections is of a prank played at a local police department many years ago. A veteran officer had been assigned to answer phones in the communications center during his last years before retiring. Answering calls from the public can be difficult. People call the police for just about everything, from weather reports to school closings to the Minnesota Twins game score.

All the years on the job had made this veteran bitter, and the new assignment was frustrating. One spring day, his friends decided to play a practical joke on him. A fellow officer called and, disguising his voice as an elderly woman, asked, "Yes, officer, do you know if it is safe to walk across the ice at Lake James this time of year?"

"Yes, lady," the veteran retorted angrily. "It is safe to walk across the ice, and don't ever call the police again to ask such a foolish question." He slammed the phone down and hollered for everyone to hear, "Now they are calling us to ask if the ice is safe. What next?"

When another call came into the department twenty minutes later, the veteran's friends made sure he took the call. It was a caller reporting that an old lady had just fallen through the ice at Lake James.

As the officer frantically prepared to dispatch every emergency vehicle in the city, his friends let him in on the joke.

Another favorite memory is about a young police officer who was always anxious to be first on the scene. He tried hard to do things right, but his lack of experience and overeagerness sometimes conspired against him. One day, he and his partner were called to a burglary scene. Upon arrival, the new officer bolted from the squad car and hurried to the address reporting the call. A woman met him on the front steps.

"Are you the woman that reported the burglary?" he asked.

"Yes—"

The eager officer stepped past her and walked briskly into the home. He scanned the residence and said, "My God, lady, they really gutted this place out, didn't they? What a disaster!"

The shocked woman replied, "I was calling about the neighbor's house."

There was no way to recover from his embarrassment. The new officer waited in the car while his partner took the woman's report.

The Clever

Clever offenders always catch the attention of a warden. These convicts use their cunning and intelligence to become "better" inmates—that is, inmates skilled at breaking rules and disrupting order. They are crafty and potentially dangerous, and their conniving makes unraveling their latest scheme a constant priority.

At Oak Park Heights, segregated inmates are forbidden from communicating with other inmates in the facility. Once, an inmate housed in Segregation wanted to contact someone in the living unit and devised a clever solution to the problem. He sent a letter—not addressed to the other inmate, but to a phony name and address outside. For a return address, he wrote the other inmate's name. Just as planned, the postal service returned the letter as undeliverable to the inmate listed as the return address. Fortunately, the ploy was foiled when our mailroom staff recognized the sender's handwriting and intercepted the letter.

One particularly exhausting inmate was Milan Simpson. He was serving a sentence for making terroristic threats, and he spent most of his years locked in the Mental Health Unit or Segregation. He had been brain damaged as a child, and his personality oscillated from friendly and cooperative to violent and assaultive. Some days, he was a pleasure; other times, staff would spend hours cleaning his feces and urine off walls. But his true talent was mimicking unusual noises. During his many years of incarceration, he mastered the signals and beeps of the prison communications system. He even had the different officers' voices down to perfection, and many a guard was fooled by his flawless impersonations. It was common to walk by his cell and hear the sounds of the prison radio call, a certain guard speaking, or a television dialogue—only to learn it was just Milan.

One of the most cunning inmates ever was John Paul Scott, a federal prisoner with multiple escapes to his credit. Scott had escaped from Alcatraz in the early 1960s. Other convicts have absconded from the famous island prison, but they were all believed to have drowned in San Francisco Bay. Scott was the sole one to reach the mainland and live to tell about it. He was found unconscious on the rocky shoreline under the Golden Gate Bridge. Police initially thought he was a jumper from the bridge and took him to a hospital, but were later surprised when he was identified as an escapee from Alcatraz. They returned him to the prison he had so painstakingly swam away from.

Many years after this dramatic escape attempt, Scott came to Oak Park Heights for a stay. He was an elderly man with a gentle demeanor, but we knew he was as slippery as a snake and watched him closely. One day we were unable to account for him. Inmates are counted many times a day, and this particular day the count didn't clear. The missing inmate was John Paul Scott. This harrowing discovery sent shock waves throughout the prison and a frantic search began—until someone realized he was in the barbershop, exactly where he was supposed to be. It was all a miscount.

Clever inmates are intriguing because they theoretically have the intelligence to make successes out of their lives, yet choose other routes. They are often brilliant, unusual individuals who put prison systems on constant alert. These are the prisoners who create diversions so an officer thinks a problem is occurring in one area, when the real problem is in another area. They can draw attention away from an assault, a drug deal, or even a homicide. They are masters at deception and treachery. It makes staff wonder if anything is as it seems.

One inmate housed at the Stillwater Prison was the best

manipulator I have ever known. Darryl Andrews could con anybody out of anything. He was a stocky little fellow with a sly smile always on his face. Clever like a fox, he was also as dangerous as a wolf and had a lengthy record of fraud crimes. Those who knew him would shake their heads and say, "There is only one Darryl Andrews."

One day, I ran into Andrews as I was exiting the prison and he was being escorted inside through the front cages. I paused just long enough to ask, "What are you doing back again?"

Andrews replied, "I won't be here very long."

I headed out into the sunshine, assuming he meant his case was under appeal. I was wrong.

A few months later at an off-site meeting, Andrews's institution caseworker bumped into Andrews's parole officer. The two happened to sit at the same table, and during a break, they struck up a conversation. The caseworker mentioned he was surprised Andrews was being released that morning. The parole officer immediately left to call the sentencing judge, who advised him there was no order authorizing any such release. Quickly, the officer telephoned the prison, where Andrews was waiting in the front area to be processed out. A little investigation revealed that Andrews had manufactured the entire order. Between manufacturing the paperwork and forging signatures, he had almost completed a magnificent hoax on the criminal justice system. Pure coincidence prevented him from pulling it off.

Ronald Mitchell was an inmate who actually succeeded with a clever scheme. A slender man in his late teens, he had terrorized the Wisconsin prison system before being transferred to Oak Park Heights. He was an ingenious man with a penchant for boating, and the creative plot he carried out while housed in our Segregation Unit is unprecedented.

I received the telephone call at home on a Saturday morning. The prison watch commander started the conversation by saying, "Sit down, because you're not going to believe what I'm about to tell you." I found a seat and he then related a bizarre tale.

Mitchell had used towels, washcloths, and magazines to plug all the crevices in his cell, including the gaps under the door and between his cell floor and wall. Then he plugged his toilet and washbasin and flooded his cell. By the time an officer discovered his antics, the water was waist deep—and Mitchell was paddling around his cell on a floating mattress.

The astounded officer was at a loss for how to deal with this problem. If he opened the cell door, the water would flood the unit. While staff gathered outside the cell, Mitchell made the decision for them. He climbed off his watercraft and pulled out the towels and magazines. Water gushed under the doors and out the cracks—the flood had begun.

Mitchell achieved what few others could. He took a boat ride and dismantled a dam, all while serving time in the most secure unit of a supermax prison. He will always be remembered for his resourcefulness and flair.

The Cons

Cons are the "true" convicts—the toughest of the tough, inmates who have perfected the art of survival. They are the Big House's strong arms, bullies, warriors, and predators. Within the inmate population, they head the chain of command.

I knew one veteran con who had adapted over the years to make prison his world. Pat Ashley was rock hard, his actions and even emotions seemingly petrified by years inside. Every day when he went to work in the Oak Parks Heights sewing factory, he would move his sewing machine into a corner and sit against the walls so that no one could approach him from any direction except the front where he could see them coming. He then sat down and went about his work, quietly minding his own business. There was a reason for this seating arrangement. Ashley had served as a hit man for a dreaded southwestern United States prison gang and in this role, killed seventeen people. When you murder that many times in prison, enemies are made and precautions have to be taken. Ashley was making certain no one could sneak up on him from behind and do the same to him. He was a warrior, a predator—and a survivor.

When Oak Park Heights opened in 1982, it was packed full of cons—so much so that we had to be selective of who we accepted for transfer. If a vulnerable offender was improperly placed in this setting, he could easily fall victim to a true con. During those years, Minnesota placed younger offenders in its maximum-security St. Cloud prison. Over time, Oak Park Heights received several of St. Cloud's most difficult offenders, but they ultimately had to be returned as they couldn't cope with our tough inmates. They may have been aggressive inmates at St. Cloud, but they were in a different league at the new supermax prison.

One of St. Cloud's inmates came to us with quite a reputation. Jacob Havernoth was described as a predator and a bully. He had caused multiple problems at St. Cloud, and staff predicted he would better fit in with our aggressive population. Though not a big man and hardly out of high school, he had disrupted St. Cloud by preying on weaker inmates.

The predictions were wrong. Two weeks after his arrival, we discovered some of our cons were forcing Havernoth to pay "rent" to live in his own cell.

◆◆◆

Oftentimes, inmates who look or act tough aren't the true cons. Being a con involves much more than raging biceps and a tight waistline. It involves a mindset. Sometimes, the most unlikely looking inmates are the real cons.

Godfrey Allen is a perfect example. A murderer who spent most of his life behind bars, Allen had an aggressive survival instinct, but you wouldn't know it to look at him. Too many prison hamburgers left Allen pudgy and out of shape. Most of the time, he just looked like an old man doing his time. But make no mistake, Allen personified the true convict. He was tough, and his survival techniques were deadly. Inmate Ronald Krebs found this out, and it almost cost him his life.

Krebs was a young, well built, self-proclaimed tough guy who liked to strong arm other inmates. At six feet, three inches tall with a trim waistline and a broad upper torso, Krebs was a formidable opponent. He loved to play the bully, beating and threatening weaker inmates into handing over their canteen supplies, extra food from meals, and anything else he wanted. Staff knew about Krebs, and we struggled to catch him in action—certainly no inmate was about to snitch on him. Then, one day he decided to pick on Godfrey Allen, and Krebs's reign came to a sudden dead end.

What officers witnessed was Krebs running across the narrow, rectangular commons area toward the security bubble with Godfrey Allen in hot pursuit. Something was wrong here. A big, strapping, tough, hard-nosed offender was running for his life with an old, soft-looking inmate chasing after him. It made no sense, but it happened, right in front of officers and in-mates. Before staff could intervene, Allen caught Krebs and stabbed him in the face. Allen's makeshift weapon was a pencil wrapped in tape to reinforce it and with a point sharpened to a needle edge. The weapon broke on impact, but his message had been delivered. Krebs's reputation was destroyed. Allen spent many months in Segregation for attempted murder, but we were soon forced to move Krebs to another facility for his own protection.

I knew Allen well and later talked to him about the incident. He told me he had decided many years back that he would never be afraid in prison; he would do anything to prevent fear from taking over his life. The first time Krebs came and threatened him, he knew what had to be done. Allen bet himself that Krebs was "gutless" and would run when attacked. Allen was right—and proud of his accurate judgment. The only thing that disappointed Allen about the incident was that his shank broke. He had not prepared well enough for Krebs because he was so convinced he would "run scared." Our conversation left little doubt that Allen would have killed Krebs if he could.

Cons sometimes wield their power in strange ways. During a meeting in a Virginia prison several years ago, the Associate Warden happened to glance out her office window overlooking the prison yard. She then beckoned us to the window and asked if we saw anything unusual.

Cellblocks enclosed the yard, which was a large, square plot of grass with a sidewalk running in a neat square around it. A mass of inmates were walking the sidewalk square for their daily exercise. They walked around the square clockwise— except for one diminutive, elderly man who walked in the opposite direction. This old man was wizened and stooped, but even in his prime he was probably never much of a threat. He stood just five feet six inches and weighed but a slender 140 pounds. Yet as he approached, the other inmates separated, making room for him to pass. It was an incredible sight.

We asked the Associate Warden about the old man. "Gentlemen," she said, "you are watching Mr. Blue. He has killed four inmates since he arrived many years ago, and no one wants any part of him."

In some institutions, cons rove in packs, like gangs in a neighborhood. They intimidate, assault, and threaten other offenders. Two such individuals at Oak Park Heights were Otto Johnson and Roy Baldwin. They were murderers who spent the bulk of their life in prison. Both were big and strong and knew how to instill fear in other inmates. Although we watched them closely, they were skilled at manipulating their way around the prison.

One morning, Johnson and Baldwin were walking around the housing unit with swollen eyes and beat-up faces. We didn't think they had been fighting each other. Our limited information told us they had picked on the wrong guy, inmate William Bleeker.

Bleeker didn't look like a con. He was a soft-spoken, almost timid man who kept to himself and never bothered anyone. But he had done many years in prison for a grisly murder and had developed a sharp survival instinct. We never knew exactly what happened that day, but we were able to piece together the following sequence of events: Johnson and Baldwin went to Bleeker's cell and told him to request a transfer out of the unit. Bleeker was black, and they didn't like him for this. What's more, he didn't bow to their demands, and that was reason enough for them to want him out. Bleeker refused. While Johnson watched for staff, Baldwin went in the cell to teach Bleeker a lesson. There was an assault, but Bleeker wasn't the victim. Baldwin came out looking like a train wreck. Johnson took a look at his partner in crime and thought, "I'll have to take care of this myself." The train crashed again, and Johnson was injured worse than Baldwin.

Bleeker never requested the transfer. To him, it was just another day in prison. Cons accept and become conditioned to years of prison life. The Big House is ingrained in them.

One day, my pager instructed me to report to the prison's medical emergency area. When I arrived, inmate Les Kubrick was laid out on a medical cart bleeding profusely from the side of his head. He was a warrior with more than thirty years in prison and a history of violent brawls. Some years ago, in a different prison, he had killed another inmate.

As I got closer, I realized that Kubrick's ear was missing. Another inmate had bitten it off—not the tip or a small portion, but the whole ear. It was an ugly sight—even for an old convict, who, while only in his mid fifties, had been to war too many times. He looked haggard and worn out, and the missing ear didn't enhance his appearance any.

I asked him to tell me what happened, and his response was a classic: "Aw, Mr. Bruton, it's no big deal. I couldn't hear out of that ear anyway."

The Stupid

Crime isn't funny, but some of the behavior witnessed in the criminal justice profession is truly absurd. If cons are at one end of the survival spectrum, stupid criminals are at the other. Some of these slow-witted offenders should be taken aside and told, "You know, you don't do this very well. You ought to find something else to do besides being a criminal."

I have always thought bank heists that go bad are classic examples of stupidity. In one local robbery, the offender robbed the bank at gun point, then ran to his getaway vehicle only to find his car wouldn't start. The police arrived to find the perpetrator under the hood working on the engine. The money and gun were lying on the ground next to the front tire. It was a bad start to a criminal life.

Early in my career, I worked in a juvenile detention center, which afforded me several opportunities to witness delinquents demonstrate their ineptitude for the criminal life. One boy stole a car and spent the better part of the day riding around town. Come nightfall, he abandoned the vehicle, priding himself on committing the perfect crime. No one had seen him steal it, and he was able to joyride for hours without getting caught. Later that evening, he was arrested. He had left his wallet containing his driver's license on the front seat.

Another boy was brought in for issuing a bomb threat to his high school, thinking it'd be a good way to get out of classes for the day. His plan almost worked, except for a slight error on his part. After carefully thinking through his strategy, the juvenile offender called the FBI to claim a bomb was planted in his high school.

"Who's calling?" asked the FBI operator.

"Steve Schmidt," the boy responded truthfully.

Offender Gary Wells planned an elaborate mugging and carried it through almost to completion. First, he picked out a victim in a gay bar. He joined in conversation with the man and solicited sex. The man agreed and they went to his apartment.

Upon arrival, Wells pulled a knife, held it to the man's throat, and said, "Give me all of your money."

The man replied, "I don't have any money."

"Well, then, call someone who has some money."

"I don't have a phone."

"Well, then, we're going to find a phone for you to call someone who has some money."

He marched the victim out to the street with a knife at his throat. They went to a nearby phone booth where Wells told the man to place the call. Wells waited outside the booth and listened.

The victim dialed and said, "There is a man holding a knife on me. He wants you to come right away and bring all your money." He gave their location and said, "Please hurry."

Unbeknown to Wells, the man had dialed 911.

You might think stupid criminals are limited to the outside—that if they land in the Big House, they smarten up in a hurry. Sometimes this is true, but not always.

With its staff of some thirty inmates, the kitchen at Oak Park Heights is a precarious place. The inmates working here have to handle knives and other utensils that could quickly be turned into weapons. Inmates can only get these plum jobs if they have a record of good behavior, but like all Oak Park Heights's inmates, they are dangerous offenders with troublesome histories.

When I was prison investigator, an inmate informant, Carl Olsen, snitched that kitchen workers were smuggling drugs into the prison. Olsen was a friendly and talkative offender—perhaps too talkative for his own good. He agreed to report the next arrival, but due to the sensitive situation, we had to plan our bust carefully. If the other inmates suspected Olsen was a snitch, his life would be in instant danger.

We gave Olsen specific instructions. He listened intently; he liked being part of a plan with the guards. He had none of the usual inmate-versus-staff prejudices and thrived on assisting us. He wasn't wearing a guard's uniform but I think he wished he was.

The plan was simple. As soon as Olsen saw the contraband, he would immediately leave the area to speak to the Watch Commander. The kitchen is set back from the prison's main traffic corridor, and the Watch Commander's office is a few yards down the hall. The kitchen is also adjacent to a security bubble, where officers observe the activity of the workers. We instructed Olsen to speak to no one and move as quickly as possible. It would not be unusual for an inmate to leave to speak to the Watch Commander, and we wanted everything to look as routine as possible. Our priority was to have him safe before we raided the kitchen.

The plan was ready. We were confident Olsen knew exactly what to do. Unfortunately, Olsen didn't quite follow our instructions. When he spotted the drugs, instead of walking quietly to the Watch Commander, he ran to the security bubble, pounded on the glass, and screamed, "The drugs are in the kitchen! The drugs are in the kitchen!"

It was over. No drugs. No suspects. No arrests. The only successful part of our operation was hustling the informant to a safe location in Segregation before one of the kitchen workers ripped his throat open with a cooking knife.

With Dignity
and Respect

In California's infamous Folsom Prison, a sign used to be posted in the cellblock for all inmates to see. It read: There Will Be No Warning Shots Fired In Here Because Of The Ricochet.

When I first saw this message, I wondered if it was a joke. A guard quickly assured me the sign wasn't there to be laughed at. It was literal: prisoners who caused problems would be shot. No ifs, ands, or buts.

I could hardly believe it. It was an appalling way to communicate. First of all, this type of violent control completely disregards the safety of those involved. Second, it creates an environment of hostility, which in turn creates the need for this type of brutal control. In terms of creating a hostile atmosphere, the California prison system used to be one of the worst offenders.

Shortly before my visit, an inmate had been shot down during a disturbance in the Folsom prison yard. And just as the sign warned, no warning shots had been fired. The Sacramento Times ran the story in a short article on the seventh page. If an officer shot an inmate in the Minnesota system, the story would be headline news for months. I was amazed at the difference in systems and how prisoners were controlled and treated.

Unfortunately, some prisons do not operate on the principles of dignity and respect. In those systems, officers think that by threatening new inmates, they will set a tone of superiority. They think that by treating inmates with disdain, they will maintain control. They are wrong. Contempt breeds contempt. Mistreated inmates react with hostility and resistance. What's more, this resentment against constant mistreatment continues past the release date when offenders are returned to the community and are expected to associate appropriately with the general public.

I met inmate John Smith the day after his transfer to Oak Park Heights. What he told me reaffirmed the importance of treating inmates with dignity and respect.

First, Smith thanked me. He said that after being processed in, escorted to his cell, and locked in for the night, he was surprised to hear one of the officers say, "Good night. We'll see you in the morning." This simple pleasantry, Smith said, had been absent from his previous prison experience, and helped ease the anxiety that exists with an institution transfer.

Then Smith told me about a previous transfer experience. In that instance, he was greeted with the following question: "Where would you like your body sent if you're murdered here?" It set the tone for the rest of his stay.

Prisons do not run safely through intimidation. They don't run safely through fear of automatic rifles or corporal punishment. Prisons don't run safely by accident; they run safely by design. And it all starts with how you treat people.

This is the most critical of all management principles in prison operations. It forms the foundation upon which everything else is built. Security and control—given necessities in a prison environment—only become a reality when dignity and respect are inherent in the process.

When I was warden, I made it a priority to meet new federal inmates upon their arrival at Oak Park Heights. Most were high-risk inmates and had been locked up in solitary or Segregation—in some cases, for many years.

If I happened to be away during a new inmate's admission procedure, I made a point to visit him in the cellblocks within the next few days. This was the case with inmate Kenneth Wilson, a long-term federal inmate with a dark history of serious felonies and a record of trouble in federal prisons. I decided to stop by Wilson's cell during my routine rounds a few days after his transfer. It was a Saturday morning, free of weekday Industry, Education, and unit programming, and we'd have time for a conversation about expectations.

When I reached Wilson's cell, the officer in the control center unlocked the cell door, which opened with a loud click. Wilson had been asleep, and he now leapt out of his bed as I entered his cell. His wild eyes showed he was ready to fight to the death to defend himself. He was agitated, aggressive, and instantly prepared to go to war. I quickly backed off, introduced myself, and explained that I just wanted to talk.

Once Wilson saw that I wasn't threatening him, he relaxed and apologized. He explained that in other prisons, a cell door opening unexpectedly spelled trouble. It meant he would be beaten, dragged from his cell, and moved to another location. He was genuinely contrite for his behavior of a moment ago. In the end, Wilson and I were able to have a good discussion about our expectations of him and what he could expect from us.

Over time, Wilson proved to be a good inmate who never caused any difficulty. He went about his business, didn't bother anyone, and was respectful to staff and other inmates. We often spoke of our first meeting and how it surprised us both. The reality was this was a different place from where he had been. The dignity and respect that was preached was also practiced. It worked both ways, and he responded accordingly.

✦ ✦ ✦

Bob Watters was no model inmate. A lean, mean man, he was guilty of numerous violent crimes while armed with weapons. But even without a gun in his hand, he was intimidating, and often caused trouble for staff. One morning, I saw him walking down the corridor toward the Segregation Unit. I asked him where he was going.

"I'm checking into the Hilton for a few days," Watters replied.

Watters was a huge man with the physique of a body builder, just short of a Mister Atlas. When he was upset, the veins in his neck swelled and his face reddened to a fiery glow. Yet here he was walking on his own to Segregation—nicknamed "the Hilton"—where he'd be checking in without luggage. The staff had treated him fairly and he responded accordingly. He had admitted his guilt in a minor infraction, agreed with our discipline officer on an appropriate disposition, and was cooperating with the punishment.

A different scenario could have been a group of officers dragging this huge man kicking and screaming to Segregation. This dramatic scene would have unnecessarily endangered the officers, riled up the other inmates, and foretold a difficult future with an already difficult inmate.

Dignified, respectful treatment—even for problematic inmates—creates a safer environment for all. It is effective, in prison and in the free world.

The public is often not overjoyed by the idea of treating inmates with dignity and respect. "Lock them up and make them pay for what they did!" is the general outcry. Under most circumstances, the public does not understand what goes on within the walls of a prison, yet they readily offer their opinion of what ought to happen to the incarcerated. Dignity and respect are normally not a part of the public's concern.

Most folks would love prison administrators to make the lives of the incarcerated miserable, to—in essence—"poke them with a hot stick every day." They believe that if prison life is so deplorable as to be barely tolerable, the offender will think twice before committing another crime. Or they operate on the theory that prison, in addition to removing offenders from society, is a place to truly punish them for their crimes. The truth is, this just doesn't work—not if you want the offender rehabilitated before his release.

Ninety-five percent of offenders that serve prison time in this country are eventually released. It makes sense that rehabilitation be a strong focus. Offenders simply cannot be mistreated on the inside and at the same time be prepared to live a productive lifestyle on the outside.

We cannot choose our next door neighbor or the person sitting next to us on a bus. Since anonymity is the reality of life in the free world, it makes good sense to attempt to rehabilitate offenders who someday will be released. If a former felon moves into the house next door to me, I'd want this person to have changed from the individual who went to prison. But changes don't just happen. Only by providing opportunities for change can we hope the offender will choose to take advantage of those opportunities.

Why wouldn't we teach an offender to read if he wanted to learn? Why wouldn't we teach job skills if the offender wanted to develop an ability to work after his release? Why wouldn't we assist in the earning of a high school diploma or even an advanced degree if the offender wanted an education? Why wouldn't we create reasons for an offender to get up in the morning? Why wouldn't we give him something to look forward to, something positive in his life? It all contributes to a safe, secure prison environment, and toward the offender's eventual release into the community. The ability to read, work, or simply to have some self esteem may encourage an offender to stay crime-free after release. Indeed, the lack of these same factors may have contributed to the negative behavior that led to his incarceration.

We don't blame a doctor who fails to cure a cancer patient, so long as we know the doctor made every effort to combat the dreadful disease. We would be justified, however, in blaming a doctor who did not do everything possible to fight the illness. We can look at the rehabilitation of offenders the same way.

It is the responsibility of the state, via the warden of a correctional facility, to provide an environment for change. Oak Park Heights operates on the philosophy of its founding warden, Frank Wood, who said our job is to create "an environment conducive to the rehabilitation of offenders who are inclined to want to make a change in their lives."

Not all offenders will change. Nor would it be fair to hold the warden responsible for a failure to rehabilitate, so long as that prison provided opportunities to do so. The responsibility should be justly placed on the shoulders of the warden, however, if no opportunities existed at all.

Frank Baylor had plenty of opportunity to change in prison. He had been in and out of institutions since his teens. Now he was in his fifties, but looked much older due to his hard life. He was out of shape and balding on top, bearing the worn-out look of a man who had spent most of his life behind bars. He was first sent down for the first-degree murder of a police officer. Baylor had been a drug addict and was transferred to the Big House for drug smuggling. He is also the only lifer I have known who was brought in full restraints directly from the Segregation Unit to his parole review hearing.

Baylor's long history of drug use not only complicated his life outside prison, but inside as well. For the first fourteen years of his incarceration, he caused many problems for prison staff in his quest to obtain a fix. At the time of his review, Baylor was confined in Segregation for attempting to smuggle contraband into Stillwater prison.

Baylor's sentence made him eligible for release after serving seventeen years. This didn't mean he actually would be released; it only meant a review would take place. In Minnesota, the Commissioner of Corrections holds the authority to release lifers. Previously, this authority rested in the hands of the State Parole Board, which was abolished in 1982 shortly after the state sentencing guideline law was implemented. This law sets a mandatory release date after two-thirds of the sentence has been completed. The exception is first degree murder convictions, in which case there is no mandatory release. These inmates are sentenced to life, with the possibility of release after a determined amount of time is served.

The process for release consideration is careful and deliberate. Three years before the offender is eligible for parole, the Commissioner conducts a hearing with an advisory panel made up of administrative staff and the warden. I have reviewed lifer cases for over fifteen years as a member and vice-chairman of the State Parole Board, as a member of the Commissioner's staff, and as warden of Oak Park Heights.

Baylor's first release hearing occurred at the fourteen-year mark. It is hard to fathom that, after serving fourteen years of a life sentence, an inmate would show up to his parole review hearing in full restraints. After all that time, he was still inciting trouble. With his history of drugs and disruption, he had little chance of being released. At the conclusion of the hearing, the Commissioner made the decision to continue Baylor for ten years with no consideration for release. In ten years, another evaluation would take place.

After the hearing, an officer returned Baylor to Segregation. Eventually, after he had been transferred back into the regular cellblock, I decided to pay Baylor a visit. I had known him for many years and figured it was time to give him a kick in the rear.

First, I told him he was the only inmate I knew who came to his lifer hearing directly from Segregation. I said it was incredible that someone was still facing problems by the time of his review for release consideration. It was time to get his act together and give himself a reason to get up in the morning. We discussed the possibility of his spending the rest of his life in prison. I tried to help him realize that even if that happened, he needed to make a difference in his life and the lives of others. Our conversation seemed to make sense to him, and I was hopeful he'd think about it.

Some months later, Baylor applied for the education program at Oak Park Heights. Organized when the prison opened in 1982, this is an incentive-based educational concept that allows inmates to take classes contingent on their behavior and willingness to cooperate with all aspects of the program. I have always been amazed at the program's accomplishments. Though its formative stages were marred by troubles, including a severe assault on a teacher, devoted staff worked for years to make it successful. Even though this is a supermax prison where the most difficult and dangerous offenders are housed, the last serious incident in the program was more than fifteen years ago. Dignity, respect, and a constant commitment to help inmates learn have been the program's trademarks. Most offenders realize they have an opportunity to change their lives through their participation in this educational program.

Baylor was accepted into the program, and he became a model student and inmate. He worked hard and thrived on what he was learning in school and the changes it was making in him. Eventually, he achieved an Associate of Arts degree.

There have been a lot of stories like Baylor's at Oak Park Heights. What makes his memorable was the letter he wrote to his fellow inmates in the program shortly before his transfer to a less-secure facility. The letter explained how important the program was and what it had meant to him. It was the first time in his life, Baylor wrote, that his family had been proud of him. His children and grandchildren were now saying that if Dad can do this in prison, if Grandpa can achieve this, then they ought to be able to do better in school.

Whether Frank Baylor would ever be released is not the issue. He found a way to make a difference in his life and in the lives of others. His story illustrates the importance of programming in prisons and how it can affect those on the outside. A man set aside the misery in his life to take advantage of an opportunity placed before him.

Dignity and respect. They pay dividends over and over.

✦ ✦ ✦

The results of humane treatment are often concrete—a less-hostile inmate, a safer prison environment, a rehabilitated offender. These are all excellent reasons for treating inmates with dignity and respect, but there is another, more elusive reason.

Sometimes, it is simply the right thing to do.

A prisoner once told me a disturbing story. He was a lifer with no chance of parole, formerly housed in a federal prison in a double cell. One day, he went out for his allotted recreation time and returned an hour later. During that hour, his cellmate had been murdered and another inmate had already been assigned to his cell. No officer ever spoke to him of the incident.

This story epitomizes the disregard shown to inmates in some institutions. No, the details of the murder could not be shared; however, some type of discussion was in order. It never happened.

Dignity and respect. This kind of treatment doesn't replace control or security. It doesn't interfere with what must occur to keep a prison safe and secure. It merely provides a catalyst for a successful operation. You don't need to read a policy manual about how to show it. You don't need to train staff what to say or do. It does not come in a neat package for review. It is simply about being considerate and professional when interacting with others. In a prison, it is fundamental.

Holding All
the Cards

Maintaining control in a supermax prison involves more than physical restraints and locked doors. There's also a mental component. That's why I like the expression, "When you hold all the cards, you don't have to play them." It reminds me that officers possess ultimate control; it's just a matter of how and when we exercise it.

The successful operation of a prison happens by design, not by chance. It involves timing, approach, and making split-second, informed decisions. Everyone makes decisions every day.

The difference in prison is that a bad decision can cost lives.

One morning, I was performing a routine prison walk-through, and as I entered the library of the Education Unit, I saw an inmate watching me closely. As I approached his area, he quickly hid a piece of paper in a file folder. Instantly, I knew I had to see what was on that sheet of paper.

The problem was how to see it without causing a disturbance. The library and adjoining classrooms were filled with at least thirty inmates. I had to factor their presence into my response. Inmates are often reactive. When something out of the ordinary occurs, they sometimes become violent.

I approached the inmate and quietly asked him to show me the piece of paper.

"It's personal," he said.

Now we had a serious problem: he had refused the directive of a staff member. A few inmates looked on with interest. The ones closest had heard my question and his response, and were waiting to see what would happen next.

I had to see what was on that piece of paper. It might be gang information. It might be notes about an assault or an escape. This wasn't a power play. It was about obtaining information from an inmate who was trying to hide it. I glanced at the wall clock; it was 10:50 A.M. In ten minutes, the inmates would head downstairs for lunch. They would go directly to their cells, where they would be locked in, counted, and then wait for lunch to be served.

I tried again. I quietly and respectfully asked the inmate to accompany me to the hallway.

Depending on how he answered, this situation could have unfolded in several ways. In a best-case scenario, he would agree to follow me out to the empty hallway. Another likely possibility is that he would simply refuse. In that case, I would go to Plan B: wait. His actions were not affecting the immediate security of the institution, and with lunch fast approaching, staff could watch him for ten minutes to make sure he didn't pass the sheet of paper to anyone else or destroy it. We could shut off the water in his room so he couldn't flush the paper down the toilet. Once all the inmates were safely locked in their cells, staff could enter his room and obtain the material. He would then quietly be taken to Segregation. This wasn't about an immediate victory. It wasn't about who was the toughest. It was about safety—the safety garnered by retrieving that piece of paper, and the safety assured by preventing a group disturbance. We would get done what had to be done, but in a safe and patient manner. Remember, we hold all the cards.

In a worst-case scenario, he would become aggressive and violent. In that case, we would remove him from the library by force. This was always a possibility, though unlikely.

Thankfully, the mysterious sheet of paper did not cause a riot in the library that day. The inmate followed me out to the hallway, where I advised him that there is nothing "personal" in a prison. Respectfully, I asked him to retrieve the paper and bring it to me. He did as directed.

It turned out to be a simple letter to his girlfriend. It wasn't critical to prison security, nor did it contain information that placed anyone's life in danger. It didn't contain escape plans or gang information. It was just a love letter. He should not have had it during school, so I directed him to give it to the instructor, which he did. The potentially explosive incident was over.

In the same situation, some officers would have insisted on seeing the sheet of paper right there in the library. It would have been a macho duel. They would have wanted to control the inmate by forcing him into immediate submission, when in fact their insistence would have created a less-controlled situation.

We hold all the cards. We can lay them down right away, all at once, and feel a brief, petty surge of pride over beating the empty-handed. Or we can hold onto them—less satisfying for the ego, perhaps, but much healthier for the environment of a prison. The bottom line is we always win.

Once, in a crowded dormitory in another facility, I saw an officer standing toe to toe with an inmate, screaming at him. He was trying—and failing—to take the inmate to Segregation. It was a precarious battle for supremacy. The officer, oblivious to the consequences, wanted to show the inmate who was boss. He cared more about his power and manhood than the safety of the group. His training had escaped him, and we were all about to pay for it.

As superintendent, I intervened and ordered the officer out of the area. He was furious. I instructed him to go down to the Captain's office and, via intercom, ask the inmate to report to the office. The inmate reported as directed. When he arrived, five officers escorted him to Segregation without a hitch.

If the inmate had not come downstairs as directed, force may have been necessary, but we would have first cleared the dormitory of the other inmates. There is no reason to take a hostile inmate out with twenty inmates present, nor did we need to move him with just one officer to show our toughness. It takes several officers to safely control an aggressive inmate. In fact, it's critical to accomplishing a goal without incident.

The bottom line was, in a short time, the inmate would be in Segregation. That was a given. How we got him there was flexible so long as no one got hurt. In the end, he went on our terms and in a responsible, safe manner.

Warden Frank Wood once told me of a potentially serious situation he had experienced. Early in his career, Wood worked in a juvenile institution. One day, he was working alone in a severely understaffed area. A young inmate became aggressive, destroying his cell and verbally abusing staff. He needed to be removed from his cell and taken to Segregation.

The boy refused all directives and prepared for battle. He told Wood, "You're in for the fight of your life."

"Look," Wood said calmly, "we can go to Segregation your way, or we can go quietly and cooperatively, my way. That will be up to you. It may take longer your way, and there may be some difficulty in getting there. However, I do know one thing for sure, and there is absolutely no question about this. At 3:30 this afternoon, I will be going home. And when I walk out that front door, you will be in Segregation. There is no doubt about this. You know it and I know it."

The boy was smart enough to see the truth in Wood's words. He went cooperatively. Wood held all the cards and played them right.

A few years after Oak Park Heights opened, Governor Rudy Perpich scheduled a tour. Frank Wood was warden at the time, and I was his executive assistant. A reliable snitch told us inmate Edwin Macalester was bragging he would confront the governor and tell him the truth about the way Wood ran the prison.

The day of the tour, Wood did not remove Macalester from the Industry Unit for the day or confine him in his cell. He said he would deal with Macalester when the time came. The Governor arrived and the tour began well. As they entered the shop, Wood asked the governor to come with him. They walked directly up to Macalester.

"Mr. Macalester," Wood said, "I would like you to meet Governor Perpich. I understand that you have some things to say to the governor about how I am running the prison. Well, here he is."

Macalester stammered and fell all over himself trying to get a word out. He was practically incoherent with amazement. At best, he put a couple of words together but made no sense at all. Wood played that card well.

Timing is everything. I recall several years ago at the medium-security facility at Lino Lakes, Minnesota, staff played their cards too soon.

The incident occurred in the open dining area during the noon meal. An inmate standing in line accidentally dropped his piece of chicken on the floor. When he was told he couldn't get another piece until everyone had been served, he threw a tantrum, screaming and threatening kitchen staff.

He needed to be disciplined and sent to Segregation, but the smart thing to do would have been to wait until after lunch. A couple of seasoned inmates would have guessed what was in store for the disruptive inmate—veterans usually understand who holds the cards. The inmate could have been instructed to remain at his table until the room was clear. Then the Security Squad could have escorted him to Segregation without an audience and without incident.

Unfortunately, staff did not wait. The squad entered the packed dining room to remove the disorderly inmate by force. The inmate became even more aggressive and hostile. Worse, the other inmates grew belligerent. Even after the inmate was gone, the dining hall simmered with discontent.

Luckily, the situation did not explode into a full-blown riot, but it easily could have. Remember that inmates in a high-security institution are used to settling their problems by violence. There is no reason to give them an opportunity to act out. There is no reason to show who's in charge. We are always in charge.

One day, a hostile inmate ambushed a staff member in the Industry Unit. Waiting for the officer to turn his back, the inmate struck him on the head with a hammer, and the man went down like a bowling pin. Other officers rushed the inmate before he could strike again, and we immediately hustled him off to Segregation and issued a unit lockup. Not wanting to get involved, the other inmates reported to their cells, and the unit was secured.

After a serious incident like this, standard procedure requires two formal processes. First, we investigate the incident and determine whether or not to pursue outside felony prosecution. Second, we assess the unit as a whole. Before we can release the inmates from their cells, we need to determine the extent of the problem.

In this instance, unit supervisors interviewed each inmate in the unit three times; they determined the offender acted alone. They recommended ending lockup the following morning and opening the unit for regular programming.

If we had kept the unit on lockup, it would have been for the wrong reasons. The assault was an isolated act by a single foolish inmate, and opening the unit would cause no further problems. Re-opening the unit, although unpopular among staff, was the right decision.

Some of the staff reacted with disbelief: one of their own had been struck down by an inmate with a hammer, and they could be next. The assault was serious, and they demanded punishment. Although no other inmates were involved in this isolated assault, the us-versus-them mentality rose to a high level, and officers wanted all the inmates punished for a crime of which just one was guilty. But that tactic doesn't work in the free world, and it certainly wasn't going to work now in a supermax prison.

We hold all the cards. When we play them fairly, we gain the respect of inmates and the assurance of a safe environment. The successful operation of a prison comes from understanding what you are capable of doing, and knowing when and how to wield that power.

One time, we were forced to make an unpopular policy change: due to severe budget constraints, the prison would be locked down on weekends. After the announcement, I visited a unit and asked a long-term federal inmate how the other inmates had reacted. This inmate had killed three times inside other facilities, but his stay at Oak Park Heights had been peaceful—so far. He said most inmates accepted the lockdown, but one young inmate had come to him and excitedly asked what they were going to do about it.

"You are going to go to your cell," the federal inmate said, "shut your mouth, and be thankful they didn't take more from us."

He knew who held the cards.

Sentenced to Life

One day, a seventeen-year-old boy arrived at the Oak Park Heights prison. This kid looked like your all-American boy with his crew-cut blond hair and brilliant blue eyes. And he was just a boy; I figured he was barely old enough to shave. But that didn't mitigate what he had done. First degree murder was the verdict and life was the sentence.

In Minnesota, first degree murderers may be sentenced to life, but several changes were made to the law over the years. When I began my career, lifers became eligible for parole after seventeen years of incarceration. In 1989, two provisions were added to state law. The first statute extended the minimum life sentence to thirty years before parole eligibility. Now, here I was facing this teenager bearing a life sentence and no chance of parole for thirty years. I couldn't help looking at this kid and thinking, he'll be a forty-seven-year-old man before he is first even considered for parole.

The second statute denied parole in certain cases, such as the murder of a police officer or the sexual assault of a murder victim. Not long after the seventeen-year-old showed up at Oak Park Heights, another offender arrived. I asked him about his sentence. It really hit me when he responded.

"I'm here for the rest of my life," he said.

Lifers are an unusual lot. They are different from other inmates, and if given the choice, I'd prefer a prison population composed solely of lifers. It might sound senseless to want to house those who commit the most serious crimes, but they are generally the best-behaved inmates. I'm not sure why. Maybe it's because they age within the rigorous control of a prison. Over the years, they seem to mature into acceptance of their situation. Many take on a leadership role, setting a positive example of compliance for other inmates.

Such was the case with lifer Theodore M. Walsh. He had been on death row in a Florida prison, and boasted the incredible credentials of having escaped from prison while awaiting his execution. His capture ensured that he would never be free again. He was now doing time at Oak Park Heights on an interstate transfer.

Walsh was an interesting character. A massive, powerful man, he had grown soft and flabby during his long years in a cell. Still, he always wore a smile and was pleasant to be around—even if he was a murderer who had once been sentenced to death for his crime. As warden, I knew Walsh well during his stay at Oak Park Heights. He made many positive changes in his life, even as the years in prison took their toll on his health. He always found a way to aid other offenders. He helped them in school, counseled them in the units, and set an example of how to turn the drudgery of years in prison into something positive.

When Oak Park Heights implemented the Choices program a few years ago, it seemed tailor-made for Walsh. Choices was an innovative counseling program that brought high-risk juvenile delinquents from a state and county correctional facility into the prison. For two-hour sessions on five consecutive Tuesdays, offenders educated the juveniles about life in prison and counseled them to make the right choices. Each of the five sessions focused on a specific message. The five or six offenders involved in the program had spent the majority of their lives in prison. They had little hope of release, and several, including Walsh, faced life without chance of parole. Under controlled and secure conditions, these dangerous offenders valiantly attempted to convince the youngsters they had choices in life—including the choice to stay out of prison.

From the beginning, Walsh threw himself into the program. His talks were incredible, and he was passionate in his conviction that he could get the kids on the right track. He told the juveniles about his life, the many mistakes he made, and where they led him. He compared the choice to stay crime-free to other choices in life. "If you were told to quit eating a certain vegetable because it was killing you," he argued, "you'd stop." But, he said, they didn't seem able to stop doing something else that would kill them. He told these juvenile delinquents that they each had "criminal cancer" and would die in prison. They ingest it everyday, he said, and it would ultimately lead to their death—unless they chose to stay crime-free. They listened and they learned from Ted Walsh.

He told them about the directives, the memos, the rules, the regulations, the policies, the procedures, and all that goes with the loss of control in prison. He described the memo notifying inmates that the entire prison would be locked on Christmas Day and the closed-circuit television in the cells would air nothing but *It's a Wonderful Life*, starring Jimmy Stewart—just one less choice in prison.

Over the years, Walsh's health worsened, preventing him from continuing with the program. In 2000, he was diagnosed with stomach cancer and sent to the prison's Medical Ward. As he came closer to death, he asked me when he could get back to work with "the kids." He never made it. He truly loved the program and the troubled youngsters, and felt he was really helping to change some young lives.

Of course, not all lifers mature and change in prison. Inmate Roland Olson was a prime example. A double murderer with a life sentence staring back at him, he was tall, well-built, and imposing, which caused you to shrink back by his mere presence. It was my duty to tell him of a new state law requiring him to pay a portion of his institutional wages into a victims restitution fund. He glared back at me and then asked, "Let me see if I understand this correctly. The law is going to take some of the wages I earn in prison, and this money is going to be sent to victims. Is that right?" When I said yes, he grew angry. "I don't think that's fair. My victims are all dead."

Lifer Elton Gray was another hard case with a warped perspective on human life. I served on a parole panel for Gray, an expressionless man who appeared never to have smiled in his life. He was serving a life sentence at the Minnesota Correctional Facility-Faribault for the rape and murder of a teenage girl. His sentence required him to be eligible for parole after serving seventeen years.

At the hearing, Gray was asked to review his crime. Accordingly, he described plotting the attack. He waited outside the pizza parlor where the victim and a teenage boy were closing up. "I thought about killing the boy," Gray said, but he decided to wait patiently until the boy had finished work and left the girl all alone. This statement brought a chill into the room, not so much for what he said as the way he said it. He spoke without emotion, merely explaining the sequence of events. He spared the boy's life, not out of compassion, but because it was more practical to his purposes to wait. He wanted to rape and murder the girl, and if he had killed the boy, it would have been merely a necessity to get to the girl.

"I thought about killing the boy." It was said in the same way as one might say, "I thought about going to the store." He showed no sense of guilt or remorse, no sensation at all. The boy's life meant nothing to Gray.

I have often thought of the boy in the pizza parlor that evening. His life was spared and he never even suspected it. Someone waited outside in the dark debating whether or not to kill him, then casually decided to let him live. I wonder, had he been present at that hearing, how he would have reacted to Gray's comment. I wonder what he would think, knowing how little consideration had gone into the decision to let him live the rest of his life.

After Gray finished describing his crime, the panel allowed him a closing statement. This is an inmate's opportunity to make a final plea for his release. Many inmates reiterate their belief that they are a different person now than when they came to prison. They talk about their support systems in the community or their good conduct record in prison. They show off a diploma or a record of attendance in therapy groups.

If any of the panel members were still considering Gray's release, he sealed his fate with his closing remarks. Though Gray spoke with candid honesty, he did not make any of the usual claims. Instead, he simply said, "I might do this again."

His statement was bloodcurdling. The mere thought of releasing Gray into an unsuspecting community made me shudder.

I have heard many merciless comments from inmates, but none stay with me like Gray's. None have the magnitude of his statement. Gray was in a category by himself.

The panel did not struggle with long deliberations or conflicting opinions. Releasing Gray was out of the question. His sentence was continued for ten years with no consideration for release. I wonder what he will say at his next parole hearing.

✦✦✦

Gray is not the only lifer who has amazed me with his comments. What particularly shocks me are the rationalizations killers use to justify what they have done. The coldness of their remarks reminds me why they are incarcerated.

One murderer concluded the detailed description of his executions by saying, "You know what happens when you get pissed off." He actually thought the parole board would identify with the murderous anger that led him to kill five people, three of them children. He thought we would understand—he was just "pissed off."

Lifer Roger Brooks was another inmate with a twisted sense of reason. He thought nothing of approaching a group of minority offenders and calling them every racial slur in the book. As a result, he spent the majority of his time in protective custody. Brooks also practiced self-mutilation and routinely cut open his arms and legs. Once, he got hold of a razor blade, slashed deep cuts in his thighs, then stuck pencils and paperclips in the wounds.

Brooks, who was serving time for armed robbery, argued to the parole board that his sentence should have been mitigated because he had carried the gun while his accomplice went unarmed and got a lighter sentence. Brooks said he didn't want the gun in the hands of his accomplice because he was "nuts."

Brooks also argued that he had "saved the life" of his robbery victim. When I asked him to explain, he said that when he ran out of the store, the store owner chased him; by virtue of the fact that he decided not to shoot the man, he saved his life. I suppose that is one way of looking at it. The parole board didn't see it that way.

Another man told me the murder of his wife should have been ruled a suicide. Since he admitted he shot and killed her,

I asked him to explain his logic. His reason was simple. "Any woman," he said, "that would deliberately get her husband so angry that he would choose to take a shotgun and kill her, would have known what she was doing, and how her husband would respond." Therefore, he argued, she had angered him deliberately to the point that her life was in danger, and the murder should have been ruled a suicide.

Like I said, lifers are different. They commit, for the most part, unusual crimes, often without prior criminal history. Their logic can be skewed.

During a parole hearing a few years ago, a serial murderer with a bloody trail of victims across several states made a comment I will always remember. It wasn't gruesome or horrific. It was simply a comment that, for me, separated this individual from the majority of us who do our best to live within the rules of society.

If you or I find a parking ticket on our car window, we read the ticket to see what the violation is. We check the amount of the fine and when it has to be paid. We send in the fine before the deadline to prevent it from doubling or a warrant being issued.

The serial killer at the hearing didn't do any of those things. He told us while detailing his cross-country killing spree that he left a motel one morning and discovered a parking ticket on his vehicle. He said, "I took the ticket off the window, threw it away, and drove off." I thought how unusual this was. He threw the ticket away. He didn't look at it. He didn't see how much he owed or when it was due. He simply threw it away.

The ticket might sound insignificant. And it is, compared to the senseless deaths of his innocent victims. Still, his comment illuminated for me the difference between the mind of a criminal and that of a law-abiding citizen. That simple act—tossing away the parking ticket—underscored my belief that the criminal mind works in a different way.

Serial killers are a distinct subset within the lifer population. I have known many of them, and they tend to be model inmates. You wouldn't know who he was just by speaking with him. Many serial killers are friendly, outgoing, and look like a next-door neighbor. It's what's inside them—the horror and depravity they are capable of—that separates them from the next person.

The parole decision for serial killers is easy. Most have committed so many horrific acts that they will never be considered for release. They will never serve enough time for what they have done.

Some recognize who they are and, privately, admit they should never be released. They realize they must be confined forever. They know that they would continue to kill if given the freedom.

And then there are others who have committed a single murder yet their only crime is so freakish and grisly that release is never a consideration. I recall reviewing such a case when I was a member of the State Parole Board. His name was Howard Abbott, and he had committed his crime many years before I evaluated the case. I am sure, however, that anyone who ever came in contact with Abbott's file never forgot what he did.

Abbott was serving time for the murder of his roommate, Nelson Gibbs. They had been homosexual lovers but something went wrong with their relationship. Abbott decided murder was the solution and went about it in an unusually horrifying manner.

He held his former lover captive for several days while he meticulously cut him up and tortured him in the most despicable ways. He carefully went about this grotesque act, making sure the victim was conscious as he chopped, severed, slashed, and sliced away at Gibbs's helpless body. When the torment reached Abbott's satisfaction point, he reached into Gibbs's mangled torso and ended his life by crushing and twisting and wringing his heart it until it stopped beating. He then methodically dismembered the victim's body until he was able to place the bones, flesh, and organs in several small boxes. Finally, he hid the miniature coffins containing his former roommate in the basement.

Another parole board member told me of his experience when first reading this horrendous case. This man was six feet, five inches tall and weighed about 350 pounds. He was not the type to be easily intimidated. He said he read the case one evening alone in his home. As he reached the details of the murder, it was getting dark outside. Halfway through the crime, he got up, locked all the doors, and pulled all the shades and curtains. This was an especially horrible and chilling homicide.

For his sadistic crime, Abbott received a life sentence, which he served at the state maximum-security mental hospital in St. Peter. Between the murder sentence and a civil commitment as a mentally ill and dangerous offender, he was going nowhere.

Over the years, Abbott gained the unlikely reputation of a kindly old man. That's why it was surprising to hear, some years before I was appointed to the Parole Board, that he had become upset during one of his parole hearings. He directed his frustrations at Parole Board Chairman Richard Mulcrone.

"Mr. Mulcrone," Abbott complained, "every year you people

come down here and review my case, and every year you leave and give me a continuance for further review. I'm getting tired of this. I just want you to tell me when I'm going home. Even if my release is going to be many years away, just tell me, when am I going to be able to go home?"

Chairman Mulcrone looked at Abbott, quietly folded up the file in front of him, placed his pen in his shirt pocket, and told him in a gentle yet professional way that he would be serving the rest of his life sentence. Mulcrone said in as kind a voice as he could, "Mr. Abbott, you are home."

No other Minnesota murder lingers in public memory like the assassination of Carol Ann Thompson. Her brutal murder in 1963 was profiled by newspapers all over the world, and author Donald John Giese wrote a book, *The Carol Thompson Murder Case* (1969), about the sensational trial. The story broke when I was in high school, and I certainly didn't know I would some-day travel to a federal prison to interview the murderer.

Three people were tried in the case. First, there was T. Eugene Thompson, a prominent Twin Cities lawyer accused of putting a hit on his wife, Carol, so that he could collect her $1 million life insurance policy. Second, there was Norman Mastrian, a middle man allegedly paid to hire the assassin. And then there was the killer, Dick W. C. Anderson.

At the trial, Thompson and Mastrian denied their involvement in the murder, but Anderson testified he was hired by them to fake a robbery in the Thompson household located in the affluent Highland Park neighborhood of St. Paul. The killing was supposed to look unintentional, but Anderson botched the plan. The murder scene was brutal and heartless. Carol Thompson's long, horrific death included multiple stab wounds and her vain effort to escape to a neighbor's home, leaving a bloody trail through the snow.

In the end, all three men were convicted in the murder of Carol Thompson. And all three received life sentences.

Although Anderson cooperated with authorities, he never received much in return other than an equal life sentence. His cooperation placed his life in danger within the prison system, forcing authorities to move him from prison to prison over the years.

In 1980, all three convicts became eligible for parole under Minnesota law. As a representative of the State Parole Board, I was sent to interview Anderson, who was being housed in the federal prison in Ashland, Kentucky. Shortly before I left for the interview, a college professor advised the Board that the entire case was a government conspiracy against Thompson, who has maintained his innocence to this day. The professor said Anderson had not served a single day in prison; instead, he had been moved from hotel to hotel across the country for the past seventeen years. The professor claimed that Anderson would be brought from a Holiday Inn, shuttled through the prison's front door, and right out the back door.

These astonishing claims simply enhanced the suspense and mystery that followed this case for so many years. Here I was right in the middle of one of the most prominent murder cases in Minnesota history. I was going to interview the killer of Carol Thompson—the most infamous murderer in state history. I was excited and nervous. After all, I was seventeen when the crime occurred. I had heard about it for most of my college and professional career. I didn't want to foul up a case of this magnitude.

When I arrived in Ashland, I reviewed Anderson's file. His

photograph depicted a tough-looking young man, with glassy eyes and a hardened face bearing a sneering look of hatred mixed with despair. But then mug shots usually look that way, not something to frame for the desktop.

I still remember my apprehension and exhilaration as I sat in a small office in the back of a cellblock waiting for Anderson to arrive. When they ushered him in, he wasn't at all what I had expected. Standing before me was a beleaguered-looking little old man. All the years shuffling between prisons with his life in danger had taken a toll on Anderson. He looked worn out and sad—and many years past his true age. The disturbing level to which the case had been glamorized made my first impressions disappointing. This man hardly seemed a killer.

Anderson was cooperative during the interview, which went like hundreds of other parole interviews. Afterwards, I packed up the tape recorder and left.

But there was just one thing I still needed to do. I needed to know if a Holiday Inn played a role in all of this. I waited for a decent amount of time to pass. Then, when I was almost out the front door, I requested one more word with Anderson at his work site. I figured if he was on his way to a hotel that would not be possible.

I found Anderson working in the prison's wood shop. He clearly was not heading off to any Holiday Inn.

Anderson received parole a few years later and never returned to prison. He died several years later.

Generally, lifers are some of the best parole risks. Many are incarcerated for their only crime and, if released, rarely offend again.

When being considered for parole, most lifers strive to make a good impression. They do everything in their capacity to convince the decision-makers they do not represent a risk to the community. They usually prepare in advance for their parole hearing, at which they provide documented evidence of their positive behavior in the institution and their support systems on the outside. Most rehearse their speeches, dress neatly, sit up straight, and speak articulately.

A lifer parole hearing is also a place where strange things happen. I imagine the strain of prison life, along with the pressure of appearing before a parole board, fuel these unusual occurrences. I have seen many odd things.

When Minnesota had a full-time parole board, the law required the unanimous vote of all five members before a lifer could be released. I found this law to be difficult, considering the five parole board members rarely agreed on where to eat lunch, let alone paroling a first degree murderer. Nevertheless, the law was there and the process required it.

Some years back, we conducted a hearing to consider the release of lifer Leonard Kramer. He had been convicted of murdering a police officer during a robbery of a Minneapolis grocery store. An ideal inmate for twenty-five years, Kramer was being housed in the Lino Lakes medium-security facility. He had been considered for parole several times before but always failed to receive a unanimous vote.

At this hearing, Kramer was clearly upset. He presented a parole plan to live in Oregon, but remarked several times that the hearing was wasting his time. He pointed out that this particular board included two former police officers, and he saw little hope of receiving the vote. He was agitated and angry, believing this hearing was unfair and a waste of everyone's time.

After Kramer's confrontational presentation, we took a recess to deliberate. Much to my surprise, Kramer did receive all five votes. After all those years spent in prison and all those previous denials, he had finally gotten his parole. The hearing reconvened and Kramer was brought back into the room. He sat directly across the table from the panel and watched as each parole board member cast their vote in the affirmative.

When the final vote was given, Kramer sat stunned. He actually trembled. He obviously could not believe what he had heard. After almost twenty-five years of incarceration, he had regained his freedom. It was too much for him to grasp.

The chairman asked Kramer if he had any questions, and his response was one for the books. It was just about the last question anyone would ever ask a parole panel that had just granted a parole. In thirty-five years of communicating with criminals, I have never been as surprised as I was that day.

"Yes," he said, "I would like to ask a question. If the board had denied my parole today, what would the reasons have been?"

The room fell into silent disbelief, broken only when Kramer's caseworker leaned over and said, "Shut up! You don't want to hear their answer. They might change their minds! You got your parole. Don't say another word!"

We did not change our minds, and Kramer's release was scheduled to take place within the next couple months. In the meantime, he was transferred to the prison's minimum-security unit, where staff counseled him on his parole supervision. They also helped him obtain a driver's license and purchase a vehicle for the drive to Oregon. He practiced driving, and within two months, everything was in order for his release.

On the day Kramer was scheduled to be paroled, I received a call from Lino Lakes Associate Warden Bert Mohs. He advised me of a problem with the release. As staff escorted Kramer through the final steps of his departure, they made a disturbing discovery in Kramer's pickup truck. Kramer had stolen, in the associate warden's words, "practically everything that had not been bolted to the floor." He had jammed furniture and other state-issue items into his pickup. There is no question Kramer knew staff would discover this accumulation of stolen property before he left, so why did he do it? It wasn't hidden. It wasn't stuffed under the seats or covered by blankets. The property was in plain sight.

The reason soon became obvious. Leonard Kramer didn't want to leave. He was afraid of what was ahead in a world that he knew nothing about. After almost twenty-five years of incarceration, the outside world was new and strange for this convict.

Leonard Kramer did not leave Lino Lakes that day. It was several months before another release was attempted—this time successfully. He traveled to Oregon and has adjusted well over the past twenty-five years. According to his annual reviews from the Oregon parole authorities, his progress and behavior have been exemplary. It just took him time to adjust to leaving a place that had been home for the majority of his life.

It's not unusual for lifers to exhibit this odd behavior. After many years behind bars, they fear leaving the security of prison and entering the unknowns of the free world.

Lifer Bill Plant had been committed for first degree murder and locked away from society for close to thirty-five years. He actually had signed parole papers in his file but refused to leave prison. Plant was content to stay right where he was. Prison was his life. A nice, clean place to sleep at night. Three decent meals every day. His friends, his books, his television—

what more could he ask for in life? He was not going to leave this familiar place for somewhere he knew nothing about.

One morning, in an effort to help graduate Plant into the free world, his caseworker called Plant into his office. The caseworker suggested he and Plant meet the next day for lunch in the minimum-security unit. They could tour the area and see how he would like living in a less-confining atmosphere.

The plan didn't work. Plant caught on to what was happening. He stood up and said angrily, "I know what you're up to! You'll get me out the front door and then you won't let me back in."

He abruptly left the office and hurried back to his cell.

In some cases, it's not just a matter of getting paroled lifers out the front door. A friend of mine, a parole officer, told me of a particularly sad visit with an old parolee, Russell Johnson. The former lifer had been locked up for close to forty years. Johnson served the last few years of his sentence at the Stillwater prison farm, which was then the minimum-security unit. He was now outside, living and working on a farm near the prison.

During the visit, Johnson asked his parole officer for a favor. He said, "I see that my old friend, Gerry Getts, finally got his parole. You know he was the lead milkman on the farm. The job is open now and I always wanted that position. Do you think you could find a way for me to get back inside so I could have Gerry's job? It would mean a lot to me."

These stories are sad, but they depict the strange reality of a life spent in prison. These men have been incarcerated for years, decades—almost a lifetime. They know little else.

◆ ◆ ◆

Parole officers often extend extraordinary patience and kindness to these former inmates. One of the most compassionate cases was that of Adkins Flowers, who had been incarcerated for murder for more than twenty-five years. He was granted parole some years back and, despite the signed papers in his file, refused to leave.

Eventually, several years later, he was coaxed out of the prison. He moved to Minneapolis to start his new life on the outside. A few weeks after his release, I received a call from Tom Lamb, Flower's parole agent. Apparently Flowers had demanded to return to prison. He couldn't cope with the strange new world or his newfound freedom.

"We are not running a hotel," I told the agent to tell Flowers. "Offenders are not allowed to check in and out as they please."

The agent advised me that Flowers was serious in his request, so much so that, if we refused to accommodate him, he intended to commit a crime so horrible he'd be sent back.

In the end, the parole officer wrote Flowers up for violating the conditions of his release. He had been ten minutes late for an appointment the previous week. The parole was revoked, and Adkins Flowers returned to prison for the rest of his life. He remained there, content, until he died of cancer a few years later. He was at home and at peace when he died.

Managing the Yankees

I **have held many jobs during my thirty-five years in corrections, and my various job titles often left my family and friends hazy on what I did all** day. They weren't exactly clear on the duties of a Probation Officer or a Parole Board Member. Nor did they quite understand the complicated responsibilities of the Executive Officer of Adult Release or the Internal Affairs Investigator.

The titles provoked many questions, but even after I explained, I'm not sure anyone really understood what the jobs entailed. The worst was when I worked in the Central Office as Deputy Commissioner of Corrections. That really confused people. They probably thought it was some kind of political appointment that involved a lot of bureaucracy—which isn't too far from the truth.

Then I became warden at Oak Park Heights. There's a special ring to that title, warden. It's a powerful word, like "Alcatraz," "the Rock," or "maximum security"—all words with bite.

I liked to explain the job change with an analogy. "Before," I told my friends and family, "I worked in the Commissioner of Baseball's office as a Deputy Commissioner, managing various aspects of major league baseball." There's a job description that would even mystify baseball purists and most assuredly the general public. I'd pause, then say "Now, I'm managing the Yankees."

Everyone knew what that meant. It meant being in charge of the most famous baseball team ever—with all the pressure and expectations that job demanded.

And being warden at Oak Park Heights meant running one of the most famous prisons in the world.

✦✦✦

What was it like to be in charge in this strange world of supermax prisons and high-profile criminals? I'll say this, it wasn't easy.

No family vacation ever went uninterrupted by a telephone call from the prison. I couldn't sit down to watch the Super Bowl or help my grandchildren unwrap their Christmas presents without worrying when a call would come. The hotel room telephone light never blinked with a positive message. At home, no call from the prison ever brought good news. No one paged at two o'clock in the morning to say things were going well. I could never escape the pressures of the job; it was a full-time responsibility, twenty-four hours a day, seven days a week.

When the pager was invented years ago, it was a skinny, funny-looking piece of equipment, much different from the sleek gadgets of today. It looked like a steel rod clipped to your belt, and there was no vibration option. When a page came, the whole world knew about it. The dictates of the job did not allow me to turn it off, and my pager sounded in the middle of my back swing on the golf course, in the movie theater, at dinner in a restaurant. One time, it went off when I was attending an event at my child's school. We were seated in the middle of the crowded auditorium, in the middle of the row, listening to a fourth grader read a poem. My pager sounded. It started with several quick, short, loud beeps in a row. Next came the static, like on walkie-talkies, that seemed to go on forever. Finally came the caller's voice: "Jim Bruton, call the prison immediately." As I stood up and worked my way out of the row, I was sure everyone thought I was a felon on work release or day furlough.

When I was Deputy Commissioner, I had one particularly bad day. The pager went off about every minute all morning long. I needed a break and decided to take it into the restroom with the sports page. I just got comfortable when the pager went off again. Back in my office, I told my secretary I was going to throw that pager through the window and enjoy watching the glass break. Then I would go out to the parking lot and stand over the pager until a truck came by and drove over it. Then I would grind it under my shoe until it was mixed into the blacktop. Finally, I would enjoy looking at the spot when I came to work every day.

Karen Lueken, my secretary, is a wonderful person. While I ranted and raved, she listened patiently. When I finished, she politely said, "Why don't you just shut it off?"

Sadly, I couldn't.

Weekends and holidays didn't bring much relief from work responsibilities. Saturday and Sunday often meant more phone calls, and I routinely went in to catch up on paperwork and make rounds. And I never missed a holiday at the prison. It was my practice to go in every Thanksgiving and Christmas to recognize staff for being away from their families. I went in every shift, three times a day, to make sure each staff member felt appreciated. It was as important as anything I did as warden.

I was never truly separated from the prison. It got to the point where every time the phone rang, even if it didn't turn out to be the prison, my mind would be back inside the walls, the razor ribbon, the magnificent complex that housed the most violent and dangerous of the world's prisoners.

✦✦✦

A couple of months after I retired, I was playing golf—one of my favorite pastimes—and I got a hole in one. It was my first ever, and the golf course sent my name to the local newspaper. When the article ran, I commented to a friend that it was the first time I had seen my name in print in connection with something good. In the past, my name always appeared in the same paragraph with a serial killer, drug dealer, murderer, or rapist.

Working in a prison is like entering the Twilight Zone every day. You wake up in the morning, shower, and get ready for work. All very normal. You get into your car and drive to work. Normal. You turn onto the manicured prison grounds, park your car, and walk to the front door. Normal. Then you enter this strange place and your world turns upside down.

The us-versus-them mindset starts when you walk in the front door. Most of your wards have killed at least one person; the rest are rapists and thieves. These people kill, maim, assault, rape, steal, manipulate, extort, and in general live a violent lifestyle. Some would take a life over a lost card game or a stolen candy bar. It is a work environment filled with lies, misrepresentations, and con games. You never know what is real. You always suspect a diversion. You get caught up in a game—one that is critical for you to win. The doors, locks, security, uniforms, stairs, long corridors, bars, fences, razor ribbon, handcuffs, restraints, mace, pepper gas, suicide gowns—it's all here, inside the walls, waiting for you every day. I worked in this environment for many years and learned every single day. Sometimes it saddened me; other times I just shook my head in disbelief.

On the outside, a bar of soap is for washing. Inside, it becomes a weapon, deadly if hidden in a sock and swung at someone's head.

Outside, string is for tying packages. Inside, it becomes a means to pass contraband under doors and between cells.

Outside, toothpaste is for brushing teeth. Inside, it becomes adhesive for covering hiding spaces in walls.

Outside, television is for relaxing in front of a program. Inside, it becomes a cache for weapons and drugs; prison televisions now have clear cases so the inside parts are always in full view.

Outside, leftover food is for snacking. Inside, it becomes the base product of homemade alcohol.

Outside, a microwave oven is for warming a meal. Inside, it becomes a tool for heating liquid to the boiling point. I once watched the skin peel off an inmate's face after a fellow prisoner threw microwaved soup at him.

In this work environment, sometimes you have to go on gut instinct. That means never turning your back on certain inmates, such as Jim Morgan. He was a multiple murderer who seemed to contain a pent-up hatred for anyone in authority. His eyes were like cold steel, and even his body movements were unnatural, like an animal set to pounce. I didn't trust him from the day I met him. He had his share of trouble in prison, and perhaps that was one of the reasons I felt the way I did about him. Mostly, though, it was just a coldness I felt around him, like human life meant nothing to him. I have asked other officers what they thought about Morgan, and some feel the same way I do, while others think of him as just another inmate. When I was around him, however, I always made sure I knew where he was. The prison probably contained more dangerous men than Morgan, but I never found another inmate that bothered me as much.

Even the simple act of sending a memo is different in this

environment. Few executives write a memo several times and make seven or eight staff members edit it before sending it out. Some memos take weeks to write, even though they are no more than a few lines. When you are sending a message to violent offenders, you don't want any misunderstandings.

It was arduous, demanding work, but it sure was interesting. Sometimes, I took grief for things I had no control over, but occasionally I got credit for something I didn't do. One of my favorite moments was when inmate Gerry Cook was transferred to the Industry Unit. He had been on the waiting list for a time, and one morning as I was making rounds, he approached me complaining his transfer should have happened by now. I told him I would look into it, jotted myself a note, and put it in my pocket. I had every intention of checking into it when I returned to my office. About an hour later, I was still making rounds when I spotted Cook being moved into the Industry Unit with his belongings. Cook saw me and said, "Thanks a lot, Warden. I appreciate you getting me transferred."

I hadn't done a thing. The transfer had been in the works, and he simply got moved as the schedule dictated. But I just smiled and nodded as I walked by. I probably should have told him the truth, but it felt too good.

One of my favorite stories is a fable about a warden who retired and gave a gift to his replacement. The old warden had been around for years and had experienced many joys and difficulties during his tenure. On his last day, the new warden arrived and moved in some office essentials. Before leaving, the old warden quietly wished his successor well and handed him three sealed and numbered envelopes.

"Someday," he said, "you'll be in trouble here. When you are, and things are looking bad, think about the envelopes. There may be some advice in them to help you."

The new warden thanked him then tossed the envelopes into his bottom desk drawer. They didn't seem significant at the time.

The new warden's "honeymoon" was wonderful. The prison was quiet and he enjoyed his new responsibilities. Then things started going wrong. Prisoners began committing assaults and smuggling in drugs. Finally, there was a massive escape: four murderers serving life sentences absconded and terrorized the city.

It was a bad incident that brought lots of press, none good. A news conference was scheduled. The warden knew his job was in jeopardy. As reporters gathered in the conference room, he sat at his desk, nervous and depressed, certain that a great career was about to end.

Then he remembered the gift from the old warden. He reached into the bottom drawer and found the envelope marked "Number 1." He tore it open and found a small piece of paper that read, "Blame your predecessor."

He walked calmly into the media room and told the reporters of the mess he had inherited. He said the previous administration had done a poor job running the prison, and it had taken his first months to straighten things out. The escapes, he said, were an example of the problems he had faced upon arrival, and they did not reflect the current positive operations of the prison.

It worked. The media bought it. His superiors bought it. Instead of facing humiliation, he came out a hero. He had cleaned up the prison. It was now obvious to everyone that his arrival was a good thing, and the prison was moving forward. The escapes seemed to vanish from everyone's mind. Things seemed even better than before. The old warden's advice had been well-received, and best of all, there were two more envelopes if ever needed.

Several months passed, and the prison looked better every day. The new warden seemed solidly entrenched in the leadership role when suddenly another nightmare occurred. A two-day battle over drugs and weapons ended in multiple inmate homicides.

Once again, media swarmed the prison. It would be difficult to survive the bad press, and it looked like it was all over for the new boss. He was in turmoil. As the media set up in the conference room, he remembered the envelopes. He raced to his desk, opened the bottom drawer, and removed envelope "Number 2." He ripped it open and took out a small piece of paper bearing a single word. It read, "Reorganize."

The new warden went into the news conference and, with the cameras rolling, fired the captain of security and both his associate wardens. He then announced the promotion of the governor's nephew to captain and promoted two legislative leaders' relatives to the other posts. It was a monumental decision. He publicly ridded the prison of all staff connected to the previous administration, and vowed new leadership and direction during the tough times ahead.

It worked again. He was recognized for his tough decision-making during the most trying of times. He was in solid with the governor's office and the legislature, and was thought to be a bold leader. Once again, the old warden had come through for him. There was a burst of confidence like never before. And there was still another envelope.

Several more months passed quietly then a massive riot rocked the prison. Assaults, escapes, and severe damage sent the prison out of control for several days.

When the riot was over, the media was back. It was again time for concern about the warden's future, but now he wasn't worried. In fact, he felt bolstered with confidence for the future, because lying on his desk was the third envelope. It would, once again, contain expert advice. He hadn't even called his superiors this time. He just knew it would all work out as before. He would simply follow the advice in the envelope. It was a sure a thing. A cinch. A done deal.

The media was waiting, and he was ready for them. As he walked to the door to enter the conference room, he opened the last envelope, prepared to follow the advice from the old warden. The piece of paper read, "Make three envelopes."

I was fortunate. I never had to use any envelopes.

I believe in trying to make a difference. One reason I liked my job as warden so much was that I had the opportunity to make a difference every single day. In a supermax prison like Oak Park Heights, the warden holds tremendous power. The audience is always captive. When the warden speaks, everyone listens. When the warden walks around the prison, everyone takes notice. A shift lieutenant once told me that he not only knew when I was inside the prison, he knew the moment my car turned into the prison driveway.

When this kind of power accompanies a job, believe me, you have the opportunity to make a difference. A word of encouragement or a special thank you from the warden makes an important statement. "Thanks for the good report," I often said to a staff person, or to an inmate, "Congratulations" on completing a class or degree. I was incredibly fortunate to work every day with officers and staff who were the best of the best—highly trained and committed, confident and compassionate, worthy of the highest esteem.

I loved the job. It was challenging, fascinating, unusual, and I knew I was doing important work. Some days, I think I did it well; other days, I'm not so sure. But it was a great job, and one that made me proud. Yes, the work seemed endless, and every day brought new problems, but it was incredibly stimulating, and I never lost the passion.

It was the best job I ever had.

As warden, I was often troubled to read about the possibility of the death penalty becoming law in Minnesota. If it were to be reinstated, there is little doubt that Death Row would be established at Oak Park Heights. Because it generally takes about seven years for appeals to be exhausted before an execution, I would probably have been happily retired before I would have had to give such an order. Still, the thought of managing offenders who had a circle marked on their calendar signifying their last day sent a chill down my spine.

I am horrified by the thought of uninformed politicians trying to solidify their next election bid by determining the fate of offenders in our criminal justice system. Yet the reality of the death penalty is probably right around the corner for the few states where it does not already exist. It only takes one media-frenzied case and one politician with big aspirations to set the wheel in motion and soon Death Row becomes reality.

The death penalty is fraught with many problems. Most relate to the moral wrong committed by such a retaliatory act for the wrong already committed. I'm not trying to cement anyone's opinion or change a position on whether the death penalty is right or wrong; I am only sharing my thoughts as the person who would have been called to manage those sentenced to die and the effect it would have had on me.

If one were to set aside the moral issue and take a look at justice and fairness, you might want to start by considering the Jeffrey Dahmer case in Wisconsin. Dahmer killed seventeen people over several years for his own sexual pleasure, keeping body parts of his victims as personal treasures. Those parts he chose not to keep, he ate. Dahmer committed his despicable acts in a state without the death penalty and received a life sentence for his crimes. He was later beaten to death in prison. In Mississippi at about the same time, the state executed Edward Earl Johnson for one murder. Seventeen minus one is sixteen more murders for Dahmer and some would say a lesser sentence. This is only one example of the fundamental unfairness in national sentencing policy and practice.

Further, how can we ignore what has happened with states like Illinois, which has re-examined its death penalty due to gross errors made with many of the cases where the sentence was imposed. The worst scenario of course would be the wrongful execution of an innocent inmate.

"Take an eye for an eye," some say, and yet we don't look toward raping rapists, molesting molesters, or assaulting assaulters. However, we do look at the horrifying act of murder and answer the crime by taking yet another life—killing those who kill to show killing is wrong.

Then there is the financial cost. Executing a person usually costs more than keeping them locked up in prison for life, when all of the court appeals and such are totaled.

In the end, I am not so sure the ultimate punishment for a crime is death. For me it would be to spend the rest of my life incarcerated. Oklahoma City bomber Timothy McVeigh thought so; he preferred to die for his crime. And when he did, I felt like we lost something that we all should have had—McVeigh spending the rest of his life in total confinement. It seemed too easy an out for him for what he did. To spend the rest of your life confined would seem to be a much greater punishment than an escape from the reality of confinement.

Other wardens around the country have told me of their exasperating experiences of presiding over executions and shared the tremendous effect that it has on everyone—the prison staff, the community and the families of the victim, and the offender. A Texas warden described his responsibilities in overseeing eighty-nine executions and how taking his glasses off signaled the start of the life-taking process. I don't think I could ever take my glasses off again without thinking of someone dying.

As the warden of the state's maximum-security prison, presiding over Death Row was not in my job description, and I'm glad I never had to perform that duty. I believe I would have stepped down from the job I loved first.

❖ ❖ ❖

After all my years working in a supermax prison, I learned one thing. I could never do the time.

Years and years in an eight-by-ten cell, the prison culture, always watching your back—I simply do not know how they do it.

If I knew I had no hope of ever being released, I believe my alternative would be to spend every waking hour trying to find a way to escape. The difference between me and many of the inmates that I encountered through the years is that I couldn't hurt anyone in my efforts to find a way to freedom. They could. It's the reason that makes them so different from most of us.

After a career of working with the criminal element of society in prisons and other correctional facilities, I honestly do not know what it is like to do a single day locked up with my freedom gone. I still shudder at the thought of it happening to me.

In September 2001, I announced my retirement. It was a difficult decision. A friend of mine was confused by my decision to retire. He couldn't understand why I would give up the power, control, publicity, and high pay. My friend didn't understand that I was also giving up the pressure, intensity, phone calls, and interrupted vacations. My friend never really understood what I did for a living. He had never walked through a cellblock filled with rapists, murderers, and child molesters. He had never witnessed a brutal beating, surveyed a suicide scene, or entered a blood-soaked cell.

Also, I had reached the retirement "Rule of 90," which refers to age and years of service combined. It meant I could retire at full pension. It was time to go.

On my last day, a reception was held in my honor at the prison. My wife joined me in the conference room for the farewell celebration. When it was over, I left my pager and cell phone on the desk next to my prison car keys. Managing the Yankees was over.

My wife and I walked out the front door for the last time. As we crossed the sidewalk, I felt this incredible burden leaving me. All the pressure and prestige of being the manager of champions was gone. It was so real, I could almost picture it happening. It was like a giant, magnificent grand piano being lifted from my shoulders. It was thirty-five years coming to an end.

I had never committed a crime, never been sentenced to prison. Yet as I left, I felt as if I had been freed.

Edited by Michael Dregni and Danielle J. Ibister
Designed by Maria Friedrich
Printed in China

04   05   06   07   08   5   4   3   2

Library of Congress Cataloging-in-Publication Data

Bruton, James H., 1945-
   The big house : life inside a supermax security prison / by James H. Bruton.
      p. cm.
   ISBN 0-89658-039-3 (hardcover)
   1. Corrections—Minnesota—Oak Park Heights. 2. Imprisonment—Minnesota—
Oak Park Heights. 3. Minnesota Correctional Facility—Oak Park Heights. I. Title.
   HV9481.O25B78 2004
   365'.977659—dc22
                              2004003489

Distributed in Canada by Raincoast Books, 9050 Shaughnessy Street, Vancouver, B.C.
V6P 6E5

Published by Voyageur Press, Inc.
123 North Second Street, P.O. Box 338, Stillwater, MN 55082 U.S.A.
651-430-2210, fax 651-430-2211
books@voyageurpress.com
www.voyageurpress.com

Educators, fundraisers, premium and gift buyers, publicists, and marketing managers: Looking for creative products and new sales ideas? Voyageur Press books are available at special discounts when purchased in quantities, and special editions can be created to your specifications. For details contact the marketing department at 800-888-9653.

On front cover and page 1: Prisoner in shackles. (Photograph © Layne Kennedy)

On page 3: Prisoner in full restraints. (Photograph © Layne Kennedy)

Acknowledgments

I offer my deep gratitude to Dave Nimmer, who brought my dream to reality. Dave's background in journalism as a teacher and longtime news professional was instrumental in guiding me onto the right track and keeping me there. He used his writing and creative expertise in assisting me. But most of all it was his friendship and my profound respect for him that provided me the nurturing and confidence. He is an extraordinary literary genius and a most exceptional friend. My gratefulness is everlasting.

I also want to sincerely thank Michael Dregni, who I am proud to call "my editor." It was a true pleasure to work with Michael over the past two years. His inspirational approach and positive support was stimulating and sincerely appreciated. I have incredible respect for his expertise and have been greatly moved by his deep compassion for his work. I feel extremely fortunate to have been able to work with Michael, Danielle Ibister, and all of the other wonderful staff at Voyageur Press. They all represent to me the finest of people and professionalism.

Further, I would be remiss in failing to mention all of my colleagues and close friends who have spent many years with me during my thirty-five-year journey in corrections. I have looked to them for guidance, support, and understanding. Most of all, I have just appreciated who they are and what they have meant to me. Thank you all.

Finally, my deepest affection and thanks goes to my wonderful family who are responsible for all the support, confidence, joy, and love I have experienced in my career and life.

Author's Note

The Big House contains factual accounts of my recollections of incidents, events, and offender associations from my thirty-five years in corrections. Because of my sincere desire to respect the privacy of offenders and staff, most names in this book are fictional.

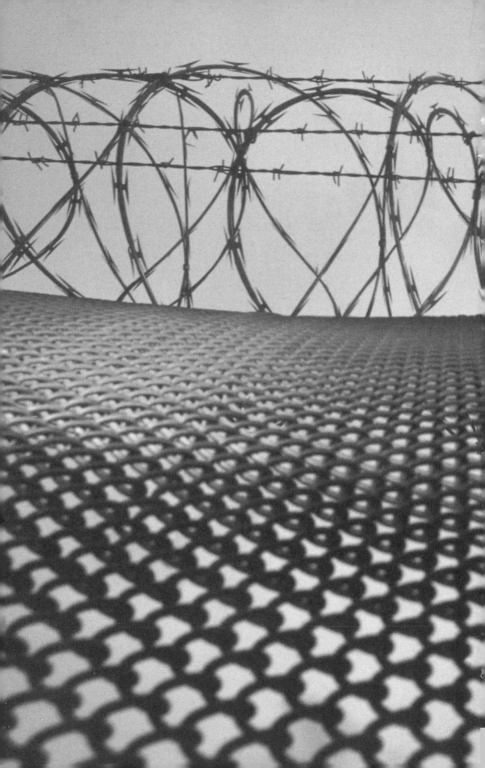